D1240638

Avoiding Burnout

Avoiding Burnout

Strategies for Managing Time, Space, and People in Early Childhood Education

by Paula Jorde Bloom
illustrated by Loel Barr

NEW HORIZONS

Lake Forest, Illinois

Reprinted March 1994

Reprinted January 1989

Copyright © 1982 by Paula Jorde Bloom

Distributed by
Gryphon House, Inc.
P.O. Box 275
Mt. Rainier, MD 20712

Library of Congress Cataloging in Publication Data

Jorde-Bloom, Paula
  Avoiding burnout.

  Bibliography: p.
  Includes index.
  1. Teachers—Job stress. 2. Burnout (Psychology). 3. Teachers—Time management.
4. Education, Preschool. I. Title.
LB2840.2.J67 1982   158'.1   82-4115
ISBN 0-9621894-0-5
(Previously published by Acropolis Books, ISBN 0-87491-447-7)

About the Author

Paula Jorde Bloom is Associate Professor of Early Childhood Education at National College of Education in Evanston, Illinois. She received her baccalaureate degree from Southern Connecticut State University and her master's and Ph.D. from Stanford University. Paula has taught preschool and kindergarten, designed and directed a child care center, and served as administrator of a campus laboratory school. She is the author of numerous journal articles and several widely-read books including *Living & Learning with Children* (published by New Horizons) and *A Great Place to Work: Improving Conditions for Staff in Young Children's Programs* (published by NAEYC).

Acknowledgements

Writing a book is seldom a solitary endeavor, and this one is no exception. Many people have been instrumental in helping me formulate my thoughts and ideas on the subject of stress and burnout. My interviews with teachers and directors of programs around the country have helped me come to appreciate the complexity of the burnout issue and the need for thoughtful solutions. I am grateful to all those individuals who took time from their hectic schedules to express openly their concerns and share their insights about preventive approaches to burnout.

Contents

Introduction 11
Is Burnout an Occupational Hazard? 11
Accent on Prevention 13
A Few Definitions 14
Some Suggestions on How to Use this Book 16

Part I Diagnosing the Problem

Chapter 1 Job Burnout in Early Childhood Education 19

The Burnout Profile 20
Emotional and physical exhaustion
Disillusionment
Self-doubt and blame

Contributing Causes of Job Burnout 24
Causes inherent in the profession
Causes intrinsic in the individual's personality and behavior
Causes fundamental in our society and culture

Keeping a Healthy Perspective on it all 51

Part II RX for Success

Chapter 2 Self-Assessment 53

Taking the First Step 54
Who's in charge?

Looking at Your Personal Profile 56
Exercise 1: Tapping my resources—where do I stand?
Exercise 2: What traits describe me?
Exercise 3: My "scrimp" and "splurge" indicators

Exercise 4: A look at my accomplishments
Exercise 5: A satisfying task
The biological factor
Exercise 6: Am I in step?
Exercise 7: My sleeping/waking patterns

Looking at Your Professional Profile 69
Exercise 8: How did I get here anyway?
Exercise 9: How do I evaluate my work situation?
Exercise 10: My satisfaction curve
Exercise 11: A look at my accomplishments on the job
Exercise 12: How do I feel about my role?
Exercise 13: How well do I handle my multifaceted responsibilities?

The Personal-Professional Tug-of-War 77
The subtle distinction between role and style
Exercise 14: What roles do I play?
Exercise 15: My style

Postscript on Self-Assessment—Accepting the Givens 82
Exercise 16: My roadblocks

Chapter 3   Managing Time 85

The Nature of Time—An Overview 85
Time management—working smarter, not harder
Exercise 17: How time-sensitive am I?
Exercise 18: How well do I manage my time?
Exercise 19: My time log

Charting Goals for the Future 95
Exercise 20: Designing a perfect day
Exercise 21: My goals blueprint
Developing goals for my professional and personal life

Planning for Priorities 105
Efficiency vs. effectiveness
Focusing on priorities
Exercise 22: My activity-rating inventory

Scheduling Time 111
Targeting prime time
Targeting time for positive self-indulgence
Exercise 23: My weekly time target
Exercise 24: My daily time target

My "Can't-Do-Without-It" Plan Book 122

Time Tips: A Baker's Dozen 126

Clearing the Hurdles 131
Avoiding interruptions
Learning to say "no" with sensitive assertiveness

Taming the telephone
Springing the procrastination trap
Exercise 25: My procrastination profile

Looking Back and Assessing Progress 142
Forecasting the future
Exercise 26: My time management checklist

Chapter 4   Managing Space .147

The Nature of Space—An Overview 147

The Microgeography of the Early Childhood Environment 149
Exercise 27: My space profile
Exercise 28: How well do I manage my space
Assessing the spatial organization of my work environment
Exercise 29: Pinpointing my problem areas

Blueprint for Change—The Critical Dimensions 159
Lighting
Color
Texture
Sound
Temperature and ventilation
Size and shape

Organizing Classroom Space 168
The elements of a good early childhood environment
Guidelines for implementing design patterns
Exercise 30: My activity inventory
A sample floor plan

A Potpourri of Organizing Tips for the Classroom 185

Organizing Support Space for Administration and Teacher Prep . .188
Coping with clutter
Coordinating resource materials
Buried under a paper avalanche?
Developing a comprehensive filing system

Chapter 5   Managing People .215

The Essence of Leadership 215
Exercise 31: How effective am I in my leadership role?

Cultivating a Sense of Community: Meeting the Need for Affiliation 221
Can I survive without an organizational chart?
Applying motivational theory to early childhood education
The concept of sharedness

The fine art of delegating
Effective communication—the mortar that holds the team together

Staffing for Performance: Meeting the Need for Achievement 234
Planning—breathing life into a job description
Training—the critical match
Evaluating—essential for continued growth

Tapping Staff as Partners in Decision-Making: Meeting the Need
for Involvement 253
Building awareness by soliciting feedback
Making meetings count

References and Suggestions for Further Reading . . 275

Introduction

Is Burnout an Occupational Hazard?

The term "burnout" has become commonplace in our culture. It is often used casually or even jokingly to describe how someone is feeling at the end of a stressful day. In some circles of child care workers, "Boy, am I burned out!" has even become a sign of valor or a badge of honor for the classroom warrior. This everyday use of the term is understandable. Hard-working teachers and directors need a code word to describe how they feel when conditions are particularly rough. But it is perhaps unfortunate that burnout has taken on such a casual meaning. Real job burnout can be painful, even agonizing, and victims of the malady find little humor in their experience and efforts to cope.

Burnout is a stubborn and elusive problem. It is characterized by a slow and progressive wearing down of the body and spirit. At its extreme, burnout has the power to render immobile otherwise healthy, competent individuals. Control slips away, the situation deteriorates, capacity to perform diminishes, and further stress results.

Early childhood educators are not the only people that get sucked into the "black hole" of burnout. It cuts across all professional lines. But the syndrome is more pervasive in the human service professions. Demanding workloads, uncertain rewards, and political and economic pressures create job insecurity and a special kind of vulnerability to stress. Moreover, unlike high-pressured executives in the corporate world, child care workers do not have the time nor the money for stress-relieving vacations or diversions.

If burnout in the early childhood setting affected only in-dividuals in isolation, it might be far less devastating. But it can multiply like a cancer, affecting the morale of others on the staff and ultimately their collective capacity to give and nurture young children. The statistics are painfully obvious: staff turnover averages 15 to 30 percent in child care centers, well above other professions. Equally significant, many potential workers are tak-ing a serious second look at child care jobs and passing them up for more lucrative and less stressful positions.

While it is impossible to put a price tag on human suffering, each year job burnout takes a tremendous toll on skilled and dedicated workers. It disrupts the continuity and adds con-siderable financial strain to programs that must search out and retrain new teachers and directors. The process threatens to com-promise the very essence of our commitment to quality care in early childhood education.

To be sure, not all teachers and directors of child care pro-grams experience the debilitating effects of burnout. Quite the con-trary. Notwithstanding all the pains and pressures inherent in their positions, many child care workers find their jobs stimulating, challenging, and personally rewarding. They have developed a repertoire of skills and personal strategies as well as a mental at-titude that allows them to grow—indeed thrive—in their roles. But if ours is to become a viable, secure profession, we must insure that these dedicated individuals do not become an endangered species. Child care workers can no longer be considered expend-able, like Dixie cups used up and tossed aside.

Reversing the trend and reducing the causes that fuel the burnout cycle is the shared responsibility of administrators, board members, classroom teachers, and college instructors training new professionals. Before individuals come to their personal breaking points, we must provide them with strategies for coping. While this task is by no means easy, it is possible to work together toward increasing awareness of the scope of the burnout syn-drome, to expand our network of support systems for individuals in our field, and to structure work environments that nurture people rather than consume them.

This book is a step in that direction.

Accent on Prevention

Mark Twain cautioned, "We ought to be interested in the future, for that is where we are going to spend the rest of our lives." *Avoiding Burnout* embraces that philosophy. The fundamental approach of this book is one of prevention. It provides individuals with information that will help them build a successful career in early childhood education. The approach is also positive, focusing on the collective wisdom of happy and healthy thrivers in our profession. In searching for clues as to why some child care workers seem immune to the ravages of job burnout, certain patterns of behavior emerge. *Avoiding Burnout* examines these patterns because they provide a useful framework around which to construct strategies for change.

Individuals in control of their lives have a deliberate game plan. They are well informed, sensitive to the stress indicators in their own behavior, and realistic in assessing their skills and resources. They have learned to put their jobs in perspective by adding diversity and interest to their lives. They know how to organize their time and space effectively, and continuously evaluate their progress in achieving their goals. In other words, people who thrive in early childhood education do not do so by happenstance. Their actions declare that they are not passive about their destiny, not controlled by events. Rather, they are active in molding their environment to meet their needs.

Drawing on the successful experiences of individuals in our profession, I have organized the materials in *Avoiding Burnout* to cover the following areas:

First, I present a systematic exploration of the burnout syndrome in early childhood education. The section *Job Burnout* identifies the various dimensions of the burnout profile and analyzes the many conditions that foster burnout in individuals. The causes and cures of burnout are complex and intimately related. An understanding of the ramifications of the problem helps us anticipate job burnout and prevent its onset with realistic antidotes. A brief discussion of the theoretical underpinnings of the malady is provided. And, for those readers wishing to explore the issue further, a detailed survey of the literature is included in the Reference section of this book.

Individuals who wish to assume control of their own lives must first have a clear understanding of their needs and their resources for effecting change. In the *Self Assessment* section, readers take the important first step in designing a personalized prescription for burnout. No one formula could possibly apply to all. So taking the time to assess, interpret, and make deliberate choices will help the reader learn how to adapt the specific strategies in this book in a personally meaningful way.

How successful we are in utilizing time has a direct bearing on our own stress level and ability to ward off the symptoms of burnout. *The Managing Time* section is a nuts-and-bolts guide to help readers develop ways of getting a high return for their investment of time and energy. This section offers numerous techniques for charting goals, planning for priorities, and scheduling that precious resource called *time*.

The *Managing Space* section of this book analyzes the subtle yet powerful role that the organization of space plays in determining overall job performance. This section also examines the spatial considerations that are necessary for developing conducive learning environments for children. Dozens of concrete tips are provided for helping the reader clear out the cobwebs, eliminate clutter, and create well-organized and efficient use of space throughout the school environment.

The final section of this book, *Managing People*, deals with the role of developing a supportive, enriching work atmosphere for all people within the early childhood setting. Many of the topics covered such as motivating, training, evaluating, and decision-making traditionally fall under the administrator's domain. But teachers who share administrative responsibilities or those who aspire to take on an increased role in guiding and leading within the organization will also find the material insightful.

A Few Definitions

Even within the field of early childhood education, where our needs are fairly homogenous, there is remarkable diversity in the types of programs offered and in the various roles, titles, and corresponding responsibilities within those programs. In this book I use the terms *child care center* or *school* to describe all early childhood programs. Programs vary, of course, but these broad terms are meant to encompass half-day and full-day programs, nursery schools, preschools, day care centers, kindergartens, Head Start programs, campus laboratory schools, church-related centers, parent cooperatives, and to include the entire spectrum of philosophical approaches within those programs.

When referring specifically to those individuals whose primary responsibility is administrating the policies of a child care organization, I use the terms *administrator* and *director* interchangeably. It is understood that many, if not most, child care organizations have overlapping spheres of responsibility, where associate directors, administrative assistants, curriculum coordinators, supervisors, and classroom teachers also undertake administrative functions. I use the term *teacher* throughout this book to refer to those whose primary role is working directly with the children and implementing the curriculum. In many cases, early childhood programs also have head teachers, classroom aides, student teachers, and parent participants who function in similar capacities. Finally, when differentiation of roles is not necessary, I use the collective term *child care worker* to describe all personnel in the early childhood environment.

Distinguishing role titles is often necessary because the kinds of problems an individual has on the job are determined in large part by that person's place in the organizational hierarchy. Even though the setting is the same for both an administrator and a teacher, for example, stress and burnout may take on quite different characteristics. Their perceptions of the same situation may be very different. Nevertheless, we should not be carried away by distinctions in roles, titles, and corresponding responsibilities. Any early childhood organization is an intricate web of relationships. Individuals do not exist in isolation or fit easily into pigeonholes. A common understanding and philosophical sense of direction can only come from a collective consciousness of the needs and concerns of others in the organization. Thus while much that appears in the following pages may have more direct relevance for one group or another, its implications are applicable to all who share some stake in the organization's success.

Some Suggestions on How to Use This Book

Avoiding Burnout is written for a diverse audience in the field of early childhood education, including teachers, administrators, future child care workers and college instructors. A quick perusal of its contents, however, will also reveal that many of the general principles covered are certainly applicable to professionals in the elementary or secondary level as well. Indeed, the following pages are packed with ideas and suggestions that any individual can adapt to his or her own unique situation.

Current practitioners will probably want to pick and choose among ideas, set their own pace, and tailor the specifics of each section to their own setting. College students, on the other hand, will achieve more satisfactory results if they proceed through the book in a systematic fashion, doing all the exercises and following up each section with a class discussion.

But *Avoiding Burnout* need not be used by individuals alone. The teachers and administrators on a staff can use it to stimulate discussion and change. As such, it is a useful guide for in-service workshops devoted to staff development and a renewed commitment to shared goals.

Remember, however, whether you are currently working in the field or as a student in training, this is YOUR book. It has been designed to be used as a workbook, so fill up the pages with marginal notes and adapt the exercises to fit your own situation. The ideas in these pages will better come to life when you tailor them to your own specific needs.

It has been said that people can be placed into three categories: "The few who make things happen, the many who watch things happen, and the overwhelming majority who have no idea of what happened." If you have a strong commitment to work your way through the many exercises and suggested strategies offered in this book, you should feel confident of your membership in the first category. But you will also learn from the experience that implementing new strategies for managing time, space, and people does not come easily. Change is often a slow process of gradually substituting new positive behaviors for ineffective or counterproductive traits. With patience and thoughtful perseverance, though, change is possible. You can stop fighting fires and handling yesterday's crises and start building castles, making goals and aspirations a reality. Implementing the suggestions in this book *will* result in direct and visible payoffs. Simplifying procedures, eliminating organizational deficiencies, and increasing personal effectiveness will produce higher morale, lower absenteeism, and better all-round performance. The children you serve will be the ultimate beneficiaries.

One final thought. As you proceed, remember, "Success is a journey, not a destination." Good luck, and have a wonderful trip.

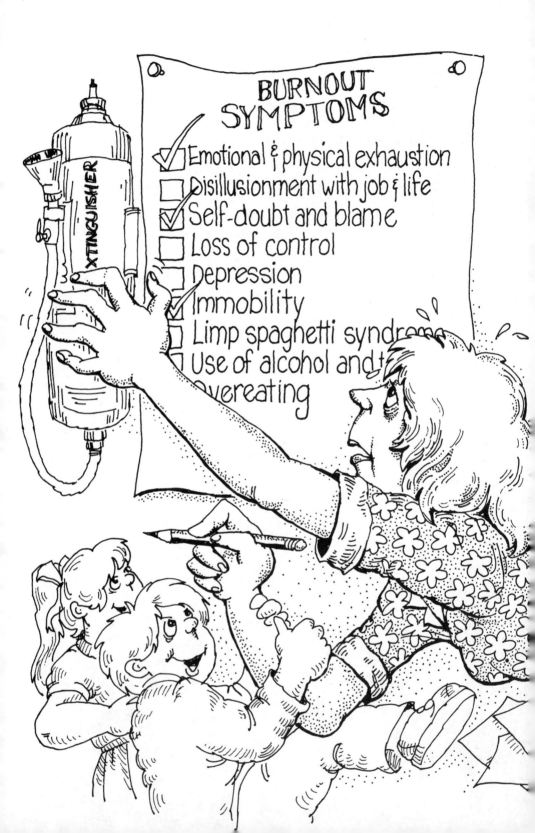

Chapter 1

Job Burnout in Early Childhood Education

The Burnout Profile

Burnout emerged as a recognized syndrome about a decade ago. The term was first coined by Dr. Herbert Freudenberger to help explain the cumulative debilitating effects he noticed in his patients who were unable to cope with severe and chronic stress related to their jobs. What makes burnout so complex is that it is not a single, identifiable physical ailment, something that you wake up with in the morning, look into a mirror and discover that "you've got," or something that can be diagnosed by a quick lab test. Nor is it a neurosis that can be pinpointed and treated only with traditional therapy. Burnout does have both physical and psychological effects that most often show up in a cluster of stress-related symptoms.

Burnout is particularly stubborn to treat because it is so individual in its character and intensity. The chronic and unrelenting kind of stress that characterizes burnout often defies individual intervention methods. Most persons caught in the burnout trap lose

perspective of their situation and try to treat the symptoms—the back pain, the headache, the insomnia—while ignoring the underlying causes.

Although the research on the burnout syndrome is diverse in its scope and findings, it is possible to draw a useful composite of the burnout candidate in early childhood education. Three general characteristics shape the burnout profile: 1) complete emotional and physical exhaustion, 2) growing disillusionment with the job and life in general, and 3) self-doubt and blame. These characteristics tend to appear gradually and grow in severity over a period of time, depending on the individual and the circumstances.

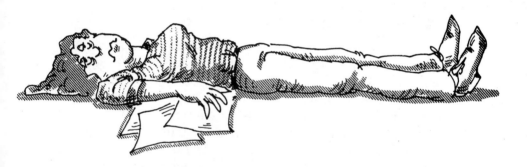

Emotional and physical exhaustion

The images that victims use to describe their stress-related symptoms capture vividly what it feels like to be engulfed in the downward spiral of burnout. "I feel like I'm a huge rubber band that's ready to snap," says one teacher, "and there is nothing I can do to relieve the tension." Others describe a sense of futility like drowning in a stormy ocean or having to move a grand piano all alone. Still others coping with the onset of burnout relate their feelings of energy depletion to images of limp spaghetti, wilted flowers or a well run dry. Unlike the muscular exhaustion that results from playing three sets of tennis or running a 10-kilometer race, individuals experiencing burnout describe their exhaustion as being a "total" fatigue from which they can't seem to spring back.

As emotional and physical exhaustion intensifies, absenteeism, tardiness, colds that just won't go away, insomnia, stomach problems, and even cardiovascular symptoms sometimes plague the burnout victim. Tension headaches or neck and shoulder strain appear with some regularity.

Occasionally, individuals will be sensitive to these early warning signals and take steps to break out of the grip of burnout. But for many, denial is the only available response. Some teachers and administrators try to counteract the negative feelings by trying harder, pushing harder, and working longer, more intense hours. They try to demonstrate that they're not really as rundown and emotionally and physically exhausted as they feel. Gradually, though, if the exhaustion goes unchecked, the feeling of depletion can give way to an overwhelming sense of disillusionment about the job and the profession in general.

Disillusionment

When the joy of teaching and interacting with parents and children slips away, disillusionment with the job and life in general often manifests itself in a growing cynicism, smothering of the will, or malaise of the spirit. A deepening insensitivity toward the children, their parents, and the institution settles in. It is not uncommon for the individual to dehumanize interpersonal interactions and begin to withdraw emotionally from involvement. A person struggling in the depths of burnout will often long for the "good old days" and try to discourage new, energetic co-workers with gratuitous remarks like, "We've tried that before," or "Slow down. Why knock yourself out? What are you trying to prove anyway?"

A teacher or director may begin to use derogatory labels when referring to uncooperative children or difficult parents. Increased irritability, anxiety, yelling, and blaming create a fertile breeding ground for carelessness, mistakes, and overall poor performance. And if the burnout of one worker infects the entire staff, then competition, hostility, and strife over organizational structure may occur. It is also not unusual for individuals feeling

such disenchantment to increase their use of tobacco, alcohol or drugs, or engage in escape behaviors like going on shopping sprees or overeating.

Self-doubt and blame

As disillusionment intensifies, frustration increases, and performance declines, the individual is overcome with an immense sense of self-doubt. Many describe this final dimension of burnout as functioning like a robot: skills and knowledge remain intact but the will to perform becomes mechanical. The workers' initial spirit and vitality all but evaporate. The faded memory of what they "used to be like" is internalized as guilt, doubt, and blame, as they question why they are unable to alter their behavior and attitude.

In addition, individuals experiencing burnout tend to consider the problem as theirs and theirs alone. They are unaware that others are struggling with similar problems. They seem unable to stand back and look at the contributing reasons that feed these feelings of doubt and inadequacy. This burnout blur results in the victims' feeling that they and they alone are responsible; that their behavior, attitude, and inability to cope is the aberration. They believe their colleagues are able to handle the same environment adequately.

It is no wonder that moodiness, depression, and an overriding sense of sadness often pervade behavior at this point. Those who hang on are by this time so demoralized that all they can do is go through the motions. Inertia, poor concentration, and apathy characterize their day. These rustouts are the most unhappy survivors. Others burn out completely, abandon the field of early childhood education altogether, and search for a more satisfying and stimulating environment.

Contributing Causes of Job Burnout

To understand the multidimensional nature of job burnout, it is necessary to look at an intricate web of contributing causes. Burnout is complex and no one reason can be isolated for it. Rather, each individual reflects a unique pattern of influencing factors. Unravelling that pattern and looking closely at each contributing strand will clarify the nature of the malady and aid the search for coping strategies. In other words, treatment for burnout grows out of an understanding of its causes. So the first important step is to isolate those causes and assess methods for reversing their negative impact.

Interviews with individuals at all levels of the early childhood career ladder coupled with general research on stress and burnout indicate three major areas that contribute to the burnout syndrome. These are: 1) causes inherent in the profession; 2) causes intrinsic in the individual's personality and behavior; and 3) causes fundamental in our society and culture.

The diagram on the following page will serve as a useful reference while reading this section.

Job Burnout in Early Childhood Education

THE BURNOUT PROFILE

- emotional/physical exhaustion
- disillusionment with job/life
- self-doubt and blame

PSYCHOLOGICAL/PHYSIOLOGICAL AND BEHAVIORAL SIGNS & SYMPTOMS

- headaches and muscle tension
- depression/boredom/apathy
- absenteeism/decline in performance
- hypertension/insomnia
- irritability/increased anxiety
- increased smoking, drinking, drug dependency and other addictions
- escape activities: shopping sprees/overeating/daydreaming
- stress-related physical and emotional ailments
- tensions with family and friends

CONSEQUENCES TO THE PROFESSION

- program quality disruption and deterioration of services
- talent drain

CONTRIBUTING CAUSES

Inherent in the profession:

- inadequate training that fosters unrealistic expectations
- unclear methods of evaluation for individual performance
- the demanding scope of the teacher's responsibilities
- the multifaceted nature of the administrator's role
- insufficient salaries and benefits
- the lack of professional standards that promote job security

Intrinsic in the individual:

- stress-tolerance level
- coping and adaption ability
- Type A behavior pattern
- the stress-prone diet

Fundamental in our society and culture:

- the tensions and pressures of living in the 20th century
- the myth of superwoman
- difficulties facing men in early childhood education
- our shrinking network of support systems
- the lack of a national commitment to child care

Causes inherent in the profession

We feel like professionals, we act like professionals, but ours is a field that has not yet entirely been accorded professional status. This directly contributes to job dissatisfaction and eventual burnout for many child care workers. We know that as our ranks grow we will gain more legitimacy as a profession. As we define a code of ethics and refine our methods of evaluation for individuals and programs, many of the problems will disappear.

An important first step then is to bring these issues to the surface, discuss them, debate them, and create an agenda for action to alleviate the inequities and improve the overall situation.[1] Only in that way will we move closer to creating a professional identity. Some of the areas that must be addressed are:

- inadequate training that fosters unrealistic expectations
- unclear methods of evaluation for individual performance
- the demanding scope of the teacher's responsibilities
- the multifaceted nature of the administrator's role
- insufficient salaries and benefits
- the lack of professional standards that promote job security

Inadequate training that fosters unrealistic expectations: Most who enter the field of early childhood education are idealistic individuals who want to do worthwhile things for other people. Abounding enthusiasm characterizes their first year of teaching, when they hope to make learning enjoyable and perhaps even profound for the children. Nearly all first-year teachers have unrealistically high expectations. When asked what they want to accomplish, these teachers say things like, "I want to tap the creative potential of my students," or "I want to give the children a good self-image." Burnout can occur when these laudable goals are frustrated, when reality doesn't quite square with expectations. Instead of inspiring children, tapping their creative potential, and instilling a positive self-concept, teachers often find they must settle at times merely for keeping the children occupied and out of mischief.

Teachers who have been trained in child development hope to apply their academic training in their work. Instead they often find themselves saddled with mundane tasks very different than they had envisioned. Directors, too, find themselves confronted by a grave discrepancy between expectations and reality as their time is swallowed up by trivia and their efforts thwarted by bureaucratic obstacles or unappreciative parents.

In many ways the training of early childhood teachers and directors directly contributes to this situation. Most or all of their formal training is focused on children's developmental needs, curriculum methods, and teaching techniques. They are ill equipped for the range of activities and responsibilities that consume a large part of their time on the job. So it is not surprising that reality often means disenchantment.

Compounding this contradiction in perceived role and reality is a Catch-22 that confronts childcare workers—a built-in, nonreciprocal balance of giving. The teacher or director gives and the child or parent takes. This imbalance is accepted during the first enthusiastic stage of the worker's new job. Eventually, though, when physical and mental limits are taxed and energy resources found not inexhaustible, resentment sometimes settles in.[2]

Furthermore, child care workers are often dedicated to their work to the exclusion of their own health and well-being. They may be said to suffer from a myopic perception of the world. Consequently, when they work too hard, receive too little recognition or reward, and begin to tally up the balance sheet, they are faced with the realization that the children and parents they serve have needs far greater than they can ever satisfy—that they will never be able to give enough.

Unclear methods of evaluation for individual performance: Self-image is intricately tied to performance and the feedback that workers get from children, parents, and colleagues. Because goals are vague and expectations unrealistic for many directors and teachers, they are left with unclear indications of how successful they have been in their respective roles. This uneasiness can generate a dispirited feeling and a questioning of self-worth.

Many things conspire to make true evaluation of the child care worker's performance difficult. Success in teaching is often intangible. It is difficult to measure in concrete terms just how a teacher has affected the development of a child or has contributed to the child's education.

Teachers often do not know whether or not they are doing a good job. Certainly the children give little feedback, thanks, or appreciation, nor can the teacher expect them to. And children usually leave the center after a year or two, making it impossible to follow up any positive contribution the teacher may have made on the child's longterm development.

Many centers thwart the director's and teacher's need for concrete measures for evaluation because their job descriptions say little about specific criteria for assessing performance. These seldom help workers clarify how their job fits into the larger picture. Criteria for measuring success are fuzzy, leaving many teachers groping for concrete feedback and objective standards to assess their work.

The demanding scope of the teacher's responsibilities: Child care is surely one of the most demanding occupations an individual can enter. The physical stamina alone required for the daily functions of preparing activities, providing instruction, supervising projects, setting limits, handling collisions, arbitrating disputes, and maintaining the learning environment is beyond what most people can be expected to endure. What makes the role so potentially stressful, however, is that this physical outpouring is coupled with a tremendous emotional giving. Teachers must comfort, console, and nurture children and still find a reservoir of emotional energy to meet their own needs. Most can handle this challenge only if the environment in which they work supports their needs.

High turnover rates in early childhood education predictably correlate with working conditions from center to center. In general, factors such as teacher/child ratio, number and frequency of breaks, adequate substitute coverage, and the amount of time of direct contact with children have a strong impact on the level of performance of teachers and their feelings about their jobs.[3] Environmental factors also, such as noise level, lighting, and places to retreat for a break from classroom duties, can influence a teacher's ability to perform.

At the heart of job satisfaction for the classroom teacher is *locus of control*—the degree to which a person feels in command of his or her own life. This concept, derived from the social learning theory of J. B. Rotter, contends that the degree to which a person feels that whatever happens (good or bad) depends on his or her own behavior has a direct bearing on how that person feels about the job.[4]

People with an internal locus of control are less anxious, more trusting, and more willing to remedy personal problems. Individuals who feel that their destiny is out of their reach and have little opportunity to make decisions, exercise judgment, and control their course of action view the present and future with little optimism. They often feel harried and obligated to do too many things for others. They feel they must always live up to expectations placed "on" them rather than coming from within.

When workers have made conscious decisions about their work and are able to participate in decisions which directly affect their job performance, they are more accepting of conditions, policies, and organizational structure. Not surprisingly, they also can cope more easily with stressful situations.

One indicator of the extent to which decision making is decentralized in schools is the frequency of staff meetings. Number of meetings alone does not indicate the degree of staff participation. But on the whole, when meetings are perceived as important by staff, the organizational structure also reflects a closer staff, better teacher/child ratios, flexible scheduling, and a clearer understanding of the goals of the center. This translates to a more positive attitude toward the administration, children, parents, and working conditions in general.[5]

The multifaceted nature of the administrator's role: The diverse responsibilities facing the director of an early childhood program is fertile ground for stress. Trying to run a program with limited resources (and therefore too little help), as so often happens, means that the director is caught in an organizational quicksand, a constant struggle to get on top of the countless things that remain undone. There never seems enough time in the day to do all the things that need attention. Eight-hour work days are often the exception, with many administrators putting in ten or twelve hours a day. There is also the unstated expectation that directors are the model professional in commitment to their role. They are the glue that bonds together the entire program. If that bond isn't strong, everything falls apart.

The child care administrator must combine the talents and skills of a teacher, nurse, accountant, planner, counselor, gardener, nutritionist, plumber, receptionist, fund raiser, artist, public relations expert, board member, and children's advocate. It is no wonder that the most common image that directors apply to their role is constant motion. "I feel like a top spinning out of control," says one director. Another describes her job as a "whirlwind that just won't subside."

The director must have an array of "business" skills for the nuts-and-bolts operation of the school, like finances, maintenance, ordering, and scheduling. He or she must also have skills in managing people, including the teachers, children, parents, and the community at large. "At best," says one director, "I always have this unsettling feeling that 100 percent plus of my time could be taken up with the people-oriented needs of this school, but there are always the task-oriented needs looming in the background that need to be done. Most often they're relegated to the weekends."

What compounds the problem is that most administrators, trained in child development or curriculum methods, are largely unprepared for the vast range of jobs associated with running a center. Few directors interviewed had ever taken even a basic course in accounting, yet the financial stability of their programs depends on their being able to budget wisely. When a whole organization depends on the director's ability to make wise business decisions, stress may be the result.

Insufficient salaries and benefits: Closely tied to working conditions for child care workers is the issue of salaries and benefits. Dissatisfaction in this area emerged as the greatest source of disappointment in several studies conducted on motivation and burnout in early childhood education.[6] Throughout the nation, wages in the child care field are deplorably low. Teachers and directors do not receive salaries commensurate with the importance of their jobs.

Despite considerable education and training, many child care workers earn close to the minimum wage.[7] As a class, they place at the lower 10 percent of all adult wage earners.[8] Moreover, benefits which can be an important way of supplementing wages are often minimal or nonexistent. Medical coverage, paid sick leave, vacations, holidays or professional enrichment days are viewed as a luxury and are not available in many centers.

Nor are the low pay and minimal benefits compensated for by a short work week. Most child care workers put in extra hours each week in preparation, meetings, conferences, and program planning.[9] In the initial stages of enthusiasm for new child care workers, the inflated concept of the job often obliterates salary considerations. But as reality sets in and the scope and nature of the role doesn't live up to preconceived notions, salary and benefits can become the focus of discontent and job dissatisfaction.

The issue of salaries and benefits is not easy to remedy, however. Child care services are expensive because of the major cost in staffing. Private proprietary centers often allocate 50 percent or more of their operating budgets to salaries. Nonprofit and public programs spend even more, often 70 to 85 percent of their total costs. But the users of child care services can seldom shoulder increases in fees to adequately adjust compensation to staff. Centers are confronted with an economic quandary: how to keep salaries high enough to attract and maintain competent staff, while keeping costs low enough to be affordable to the families in need of these services.

The salary problem exists to a great extent because like many human service professions, early childhood education still suffers from sex-based job categorization. Women occupy the majority of the positions in the child care field, and women still earn approximately 40 percent less than the average male wage earner.[10] Also the prevailing view is that child care is unskilled work, and as long as this attitude exists, pay and status will reflect accordingly.

The situation presents a dilemma for many who derive enormous satisfaction from their jobs and want to make a long-term commitment to the profession but who find that the low financial compensation makes it unrealistic for them to build a career in child care. And when they' compare their monetary accomplishments and career security with college classmates in industry or the business world, the disparity is painful. Having to compromise ideals and aspirations because the dollar figures don't match ability is a real source of frustration for many teachers and directors, and a strong contributing factor to burnout.

The lack of professional standards that promote job security: Because early childhood education is still in a nascent stage as a profession, job security is low. More specifically, the lack of established criteria for accepting new people as teachers and administrators and the lack of performance standards once they are in those positions breeds uncertainty not only about one's present status but also about the future.

"Anyone can teach" is vehemently denied by child care workers. Yet we have failed to develop uniform training standards and specific competencies for admitting new people into our ranks. Our actions speak louder than our protestations. Training is uneven and often woefully inadequate. To achieve professional status, criteria for screening new candidates as well as standards of performance once they have been admitted into the field are absolutely essential. When this happens, a rise in overall prestige and salaries can be expected.[11]

We must also acknowledge an undeniable causal link between sheer numbers in our ranks and job security. As long as "anyone" can teach in a child care center, we will have a surfeit of workers. The anxiety this creates for people holding positions can be a grave source of stress. Most teachers and directors know that there is an army of replacements ready to leap into their positions if they leave. This creates a "revolving door" attitude that can be emotionally debilitating for the dedicated child care worker who would like to make a commitment to the profession but perceives a lack of professional support.

Causes intrinsic in the individual's personality and behavior

Burnout does not occur from external sources alone. Much of it has to do with each person's personality traits and behavior patterns. While these areas may be just as difficult to change as some of the external influences inherent in the nature of our profession, they do provide an important and often overlooked component of the burnout picture. The effectiveness with which individuals are able to handle the multiplicity of stressors turns in large part on their own understanding of themselves. In this section we shall discuss four areas:

- stress-tolerance level
- coping and adaption ability
- the Type A behavior pattern
- the stress-prone diet

Stress-tolerance level: Stress is a condition with which we are all familiar. Yet the term is often used so loosely that it is surrounded by ambiguity. The word "stress" has become a wastebasket of virtually every emotional or mental problem, so it is no wonder that we are often perplexed in understanding its role in our lives. Many people automatically assume that all stress is harmful. But stress is an important ingredient in an active life. The only way we could avoid it completely would be to do nothing at all.[12]

It is important, therefore, to distinguish between stress which is good and productive (eustress) and stress which is bad and destructive (distress).[13] Eustress (as in euphoria) refers to conditions which are interesting, challenging, and necessary for self expression. Distress, on the other hand is dangerous and debilitating, affecting a person's over-all well being.

It is also useful to distinguish between the causes of stress and the effects it has on the body. Any event or condition that causes stress (good or bad) is called a stressor. A stressor may be purely physical, social, or psychological. Various pressures from our external environment like job, family, friends, and society are referred to as external stressors. The various pressures generated from within like ambition, competitiveness, and aggressiveness are called internal stressors. These internal stressors usually have far graver consequences on our mental health than the external stressors. But both kinds of stressors elicit the same biological response.[14]

The effect on the body, the biological response, is what happens when we encounter a stressful situation.[15] This could be a near miss on the freeway, a blowup with a colleague, or a surprise party in your honor. In any stressful situation, the adrenal and pituitary glands secrete hormones both to protect the body from injury and to stimulate protective body reactions. Energy sources are mobilized: breathing and respiration increase, blood pressure soars, muscles tense, and pupils dilate. All these involuntary responses prepare us for a "fight or flight" response. After the incident is over, the body returns to its normal state. This short-term stress functions, then, to help us deal with emergency situations. It is a vital part of our survival mechanism.

The important distinction comes when we look at the difference between short-term and long-term stress. Stress disorders are caused by *chronic,* long-term overactivity.[16] When the body stays hyped up, never fully recovering to its baseline level, our defense systems gradually wear down. Deterioration begins, and stress-related disorders like migraine headaches, lower-back pain, peptic ulcers, hypertension, or gastrointestinal problems may result.

Just exactly how prolonged chronic stress affects individuals depends in large part on a complex variety of factors like age, sex, genetic predisposition and the family history in dealing with stress. All this unites to create a unique stress-tolerance composite for each individual.

Basic to that notion is the correlation between stress and performance.[17] As stress increases, so too does performance and productivity. But only up to a point. Beyond that threshold point, stress impairs performance. In other words, some stress is good but too much is detrimental. This explains why many people feel they do better under the pressure of an impending deadline. The deadline creates a stress reaction that stimulates performance. But if a person is already near the threshold level, performance will be adversely affected. It is prolonged pressure beyond this level that can result in burnout.

The wealth of information currently being generated from stress research helps us understand that pressure from stressors is unavoidable. Our challenge in managing stress, therefore, is to gain as many insights as possible into the correlation between stress and performance in our own lives. Only then can we begin to reengineer our behavior and our environment to use stress to our advantage, benefiting from its positive aspects while minimizing its negative ones.

Coping and adaption ability: In his landmark books *Future Shock* and *The Third Wave*,[18] social commentator Alvin Toffler depicts a changing and turbulent world in which the very ability to survive depends on the degree to which we can cope with change and maintain a state of equilibrium. He suggests that in the coming years this will become increasingly difficult since the pace of change will accelerate even further; that we will be called upon to absorb more information, make more decisions, and adjust to changes in our lives more frequently than we have ever experienced. Our adaptive and coping abilities will be taxed to their limit, and we will increasingly feel disoriented and confused.

While we want to avoid becoming melodramatic about impending doom, it is important to acknowledge that the way we adapt to change can have a significant impact on the way we handle stress in our lives. This picture has two dimensions: the rate of change that we must cope with and our perception of the event or events. Both are linked together to determine how well we adapt.

Changes in life can disrupt our everyday pattern of living. Excessive or rapid change means that a person's equilibrium can be thrown off. Negative changes (like divorce, separation, death of a friend, an argument, personal injury, or financial difficulty) are generally more harmful than positive changes (like marriage, birth of a child, a vacation, the holiday season, or a new job).[19] All events, though, require us to adapt or adjust in some way. If we are called upon to adjust to too many of these changes within a concentrated period of time, the stress can leave us more susceptible to disease and illness.[20]

But individuals vary widely in the ways they perceive change in their lives. What may be highly stressful for one person may not be for another. In other words, it is not the intensity of the stressor that determines how each of us will react; what is important is how we perceive the event or the change. Some people are more anxiety-prone than others. They tend to overreact to stressors and as a result create excessive chronic stress on their bodies. They perceive the event or stressor as far worse than it really is and give the situation a life or death urgency that "catastrophizes" it.[21]

As individuals, we may not always be able to dictate the number and intensity of events that happen to us. But making decisions about changes in our lives and maintaining some control over how we react to those changes gives us a powerful tool for managing stress and reducing the likelihood of burnout.

The Type A behavior pattern: Research by Drs. Meyer Friedman and Ray Rosenman led to the publication of a provocative book in 1974 titled *Type A Behavior and Your Heart.*[22] Since that time, the term "Type A" has been used widely and often interchangeably with "workaholic"—that hard-driven, single-minded devotion to labor.[23]

The Type A personality hosts a complex of traits including *excessive* competitive drive, aggressiveness, impatience, and a harried sense of time urgency. The Type A person judges worth by number of achievements, and regularly suppresses feelings such as fatigue that might interfere with productivity.

Friedman and Rosenman reached the conclusion that the Type A behavior pattern was linked to heart disease. "In the absence of these personality traits, coronary heart disease almost never occurs before a person reaches 70 years of age, regardless of fatty foods eaten, cigarettes smoked, or exercise neglected. But when this behavior pattern is present, coronary heart disease can easily appear by age 30 or 40."[24]

The Type A personality behavior has effects that reach beyond the individual. Not only does this pattern endanger the person's longevity, but it unquestionably affects the well-being of family and associates who have to put up with the pressure-cooker atmosphere they create. Like some new social disease, this label has altered our consciousness about the possible deleterious effects of our behavior. The connotations associated with Type A are sure to make any hard-working individual defensive at the mere suggestion that they exhibit a similar pattern. But the key to understanding the Type A profile is the word "excessive."

Being obsessed with and compulsive about work is very different from being just plain hard-working and productive. And there is a clear difference between devotion to work and addiction to work.[25] Modifying behavior does not mean giving up the desire to achieve. It means changing to achieving behaviors that are more appropriate and healthy. The Type B personality, Friedman asserts, still has ambition and a considerable amount of drive. But it is of the nature that gives confidence and security rather than uncertainty and insecurity. Type B's can be energetic and competitive, but their energy contributes to their job and their job contributes to their energy.

The stress-prone diet:[26] The permutations of human behavior are far too complicated to be explained entirely by the food we do or don't consume. But food is a factor that cannot be ignored in the prevention of burnout.

Most people know that good nutrition and regular exercise contribute to wholesome living, and there is certainly an abundance of guides on the market that extol the virtues of healthful habits. But few people are aware that certain dietary habits can actually contribute to distress and aggravate burnout symptoms. The human body is not simply a collection of mechanical parts that can just chug on and on indefinitely under stressful conditions. Eventually parts wear down and fail from poor

maintenance. The formula is pretty straightforward: eating well combats stress; eating poorly intensifies it.

It has been found, for instance, that the consumption of certain foods can contribute to stress either by triggering a stress response directly or by creating a state of depletion or fatigue that elicits the same response. There essentially are four ways that this can happen.

First, some foods contain substances that can trigger a stress response directly when consumed. The most identifiable culprit in this category is caffeine in the form of coffee. Other sources of caffeine are cola beverages, tea, chocolate, and cocoa.

Second, a substance commonly added to our food in the form of table salt is sodium. Excessive consumption of sodium has been linked to high blood pressure as well as excessive fluid retention.

The third way our diet can affect our ability to handle stress is through the hypoglycemic phenomenon known as low blood sugar level. This can happen either through excess consumption of sugar over a short period of time or through depletion when meals are skipped. Dizziness, trembling, heightened anxiety, headaches and increased cardiovascular activity are some of the identifiable symptoms associated with the hypoglycemic state.

Finally, severe stress over a long period of time can deplete certain essential vitamins in our body. These are primarily vitamin C and the B-complex vitamins. Depletion of these vitamins decreases an individual's ability to cope with stressful situations. Deficiencies over an extended period of time may also cause additional side effects characteristic of vitamin depletion.

While the scientific research in the area of the psychological affects of nutrition is still slim, there is a general recognition that people who maintain proper control of their weight and have nutritionally good habits are not just better able to cope but can deal better with day-to-day stressors. If our goal is to operate on a more acute emotional and intellectual level of awareness in order to combat the deleterious effects of stress and burnout, sound nutritional habits must be an integral part of our strategy.

Causes fundamental in our society and culture

"No man is an island" takes on a special significance in our discussion of the contributing causes of burnout. Burnout in early childhood education must be examined to take into consideration the many societal and cultural influences that shape our values, attitudes, and the way we view ourselves as individuals and professionals. Five aspects of our society are particularly important contributing factors in the burnout phenomena.

- the tensions and pressures of living in the 20th century
- the myth of the superwoman
- difficulties facing men in early childhood education
- our shrinking network of support systems
- the lack of a national commitment to child care

Tensions and pressures of living in the 20th century: John Kenneth Galbraith has referred to this century as the Age of Uncertainty.[27] Immense changes have occurred necessitating dramatic shifts in our habits and lifestyles, attitudes and belief systems, health patterns and methods of coping. We have moved from a basically agrarian society to a highly industrialized one. Along with this change has come sweeping innovations in communication systems, transportation, medicine, space travel, genetic engineering, and microprocessing. The Orwellian future of yesterday is happening today. New frontiers are being explored altering our very concept of life itself. Indeed a label has been invented, "the techno-peasant," to describe people struggling to assimilate and make sense out of modern technological change.[28]

In any one day we are exposed to far more information than we can begin to absorb. The introduction of the copy machine alone has radically altered our work environments and job responsibilities. The mountain of paper, articles, and reports that we must contend with has multiplied over the past few years. Many believe that this overstimulation leaves us vulnerable because it increases the likelihood of our distorting reality—that information overload may in fact interfere with our ability to think, process information, and make sound judgments.[29]

In the name of progress, we have become infatuated with speed. We have invented objects that can travel faster, compute faster, communicate faster, and even make other objects faster. And in the process we subject ourselves to their demands. Sometimes it seems that our technologically sophisticated world is on automatic pilot to self-destruction. Gone is the leisurely pace and time to reflect and think. We're sucked into the whirlwind and all we can do is struggle to maintain some sense of equilibrium.[30]

To further amplify the problem, our morning newspaper tells of higher taxes and inflation, and reports a constant stream of evidence that we are living in a dangerous, hostile environment. Television, radio and other media intensify and sometimes distort our perception of the world. Most individuals, for instance, believe the incidence of crime and violence is much higher than it actually is. We have created a climate of mistrust that breeds suspicion, even paranoia. Our modern society has reduced us to numbers, stripped us of our uniqueness, and standardized us like tires on a rack in the service station.

The cultural ramifications of coping in this atmosphere have been profound. Value systems have changed. Gone are the bench marks that we relied on in times of uncertainty and trouble to help us shape our sense of identity and give us direction.

It is almost an understatement to say that we are being victimized by the pace of modern life with all its accompanying pressures. With the rapid changes, pollution, and array of other unnatural impingments that disrupt our body and mind, it is no wonder that we feel robbed of our ability to cope and become prime candidates for burnout.

The myth of the superwoman: There is perhaps no other area in our rapidly changing world that has necessitated as many adjustments as that of the role of women in our culture. The women's movement having filtered far and deep, women are reexamining their own roles and lifestyles against conflicting expectations and suppositions.[31]

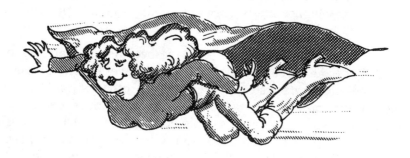

But there is no consistent norm, no established pattern or pat formula to follow. There are pressures from society to pursue a career, yet also to stay at home to tend to family needs.[32] The woman working outside her home still feels vulnerable to questions about her children. Are they getting enough of her time and attention? Are they being adequately provided for? And the woman working inside the home still feels vulnerable to questions about herself. Is she challenged enough, intellectually stimulated enough, earning enough?

These issues are intimately connected with the burnout syndrome for women. Many women in early childhood education have child care obligations at home in addition to their professional child care responsibilities. This combination of dual careers in "giving" can be a major source of stress.[33] The woman "gives" all day to children, teachers, and parents at work and then must "give" to her own children and family at home.

Moreover, because many women have less than enthusiastic endorsement from their mates and loved ones for pursuing a career, they are reluctant to delegate household tasks to others in an effort to establish a more equitable distribution of responsibility. To counter the residual feelings of guilt from going to work in the first place, they end up doing a disproportionate share of the housework. Their professional job responsibilities are then piled on top of their household responsibilities.

As a result, Modern Millie lives at a frenzied pace with little time to attend to personal needs. She is swallowed by the demands and pressures that converge upon her from all directions. At the same time she is bombarded by messages telling her that somehow she should be able to juggle these multiple roles with grace and finesse. If she elects to pursue a career in addition to rearing a family, she must be adept (if not polished) at both.

As long as the myth of superwoman exists, so too will the guilt and physical and emotional stress that comes from trying to measure up to this ideal. This in turn leaves women especially vulnerable to the symptoms of burnout.

Difficulties facing men in early childhood education: In recent years there has been a growing awareness of the importance of males as nurturing caregivers for young children. As a result, men have become much sought-after as teachers and administrators of early childhood programs. But pioneering this new professional role has brought many men stress-related tensions that develop from their special status.

Barriers and stereotypes about male teachers are deeply ingrained in our society. That male teachers have a critical role to play in the education of young children and the humanization of our schools has not yet been translated into full acceptance.[34] Men in early childhood education still encounter strong reactions and sometimes downright prejudice about their vocational choice. One teacher says that when he tells other men about what he does for a living, they usually look at him with raised eyebrows and say something incredulous like, "You mean you're a babysitter?"[35] Some people still seem to believe that presence of a male caregiver in the classroom will emasculate their young sons. Moreover, no matter how professionally a male early childhood teacher or administrator conducts himself, society tends not to grant him the same prestige as males at other instructional levels.

In addition to coping with a general lack of societal acceptance, men entering a profession that is traditionally female-centered must often cope with specific organizational prejudice as well. Women teachers sometimes feel that males get preferential treatment or more alluring salary offers as enticements to join an organization and stay on board. Women may also feel that their job responsibilities and opportunities for advancement differ significantly from their male counterparts. Whether the differences are real or imagined, staff tension and competition often result. A kind of subtle reverse discrimination may take place that can hurt staff morale and undermine organizational goals.

Another difficulty sometimes arises. Early childhood educators recognize the importance of providing an environment where children can develop unhampered by rigid sex-defined codes of behavior. Yet, ironically, once on the job, men teachers often find that they are locked into sex-associated roles.[36] They are often assigned to supervising the carpentry bench, to planning physical, boisterous activities, or covering as general handyman for repairs and maintenance around the school. Often, too, men are seen as the final disciplinarians in the classroom.

Perhaps the most prominent stress-related symptom that male caregivers face is their sense of isolation and loneliness in their role.[37] "I find myself feeling quite awkward during lunch when conversation gets sidetracked to 'girl talk'," said one teacher. "Basically, I feel uncomfortable in a room full of women. I'm very conscious of my sex and feel like I'm the token male on the staff. I'm told that I'm special and important, but I feel 'matronized'. I think my presence is resented."

Our shrinking network of support systems: Our family, friends and the network of support we have built play an instrumental role in the burnout picture. The need for understanding and support from other human beings is vital in helping us keep our life in perspective and move toward a realistic resolution of our problems. But in a highly mobile society characterized by frequent divorce, uprooted families, and fleeting relationships, it takes a concerted effort to build and maintain these support systems. Moreover, we are witnessing an explosion of "solos"—people who live alone outside a family structure altogether.[38] It is especially important that these singles have a network of support.

In the ideal world, our family and friends, and perhaps church, provide the emotional sustenance we need. They are our prime source for help in coping with the pressures we encounter. But too often this safety net is missing; relationships are not harmonious and may become a source of tension themselves.

A remarkably similar pattern is seen in individuals struggling with burnout. They usually feel a sense of isolation. They have few people to whom they can turn to vent frustration and from whom they can get healthy constructive feedback. One child care worker described it this way: "This is such a lonely job. When the pressures really get me down, there is usually no one I can turn to for help. No one understands the scope of my frustrations because they don't understand my job. My family tries to be helpful, but they've got their own troubles, too, and the last thing I want to do is burden them with mine."

This analysis is troublesome because other directors and teachers *do* understand. Many of them, in fact, are trying to cope with the same range of problems. But the nature of the child care field prevents directors and teachers from establishing a network of support systems with other professionals. Directors often feel suspicious of one another. They are threatened because they are all vying for the same children and competing to provide similar services in the community. Teachers, too, are caught in a similar conundrum. The lack of job security fosters competition for existing jobs, and many teachers are reluctant to reach out and build relationships with others within their field. Directors and teachers also struggle with guilt, because they perceive that educational services should be above petty competition and should somehow be different than other "businesses" in this respect.

When workers need to reach out the most, they often withdraw into a shell instead. In doing so, they only exacerbate their growing sense of isolation. Too often we get so caught on a treadmill of activity that we lose our ability to reach out and cultivate closeness. But if we want to secure more fulfilling lives based on reciprocal sharing and caring relationships to nurture and sustain us, we have to consciously develop contacts with family and friends and expand our circle of professional associates.

The lack of a national commitment to child care: Many of the human service professions have been traditionally viewed by the public as nonessential and of low priority. In part, this stems from the fact that the "product" is not tangible and success is not measurable.[39] In the 1960's and early 70's, however, there was a strong national commitment to funding social programs. The outlay of funds, the national mood, and the support of the general population for the delivery of social services gave confidence to those working in the child care professions that their goal of improving the quality of lives for children and their families was noble and respected.

Today we are witnessing a dramatic swing of the pendulum in the other direction. The shift in sociopolitical climate has carried with it not only severe cutbacks in the amount and availability of public funding but also a change in the public's perception of the importance of many human service programs. Priorities seem to have changed. Child care programs have suffered painful cutbacks in funding and over-all support from the public sector. The consequences of this shift for individual programs has been severe both directly and indirectly.

First, as dollars are slashed from public coffers, programs experience the financial strain in direct ways: decreases in staffing, supplies, materials, and funds for capital improvements. This situation can be very threatening to programs that have traditionally operated on shoestring budgets anyway. The burden of an increased teacher/child ratio is real and debilitating to the staff, not to mention the negative effects on the children.

Because of funding uncertainties, administrators are forced to spend increasing amounts of their time scrambling for new funds, writing new proposals, and making new contacts in the community to gain greater visibility and support for their programs. This means that program directors must spread their limited time even thinner. The over-all operation of their programs cannot help but to suffer as a consequence.

Second, the swing in public mood has affected the child care profession in an indirect way by hitting at the core of job satisfaction and morale. All people want to be respected for the work they do. Self-esteem is directly tied to the importance that individuals perceive their role provides to the over-all good of society. Teachers and child care workers have never enjoyed a very exalted place in the arena of job titles. But when priorities shift and funding is cut back even further, child care workers understandably question why they're expending so much energy and making so many sacrifices when society appreciates their work so little.

The economic and political climate of the 80's looks bleak, and the negative picture for funding will not likely change in the immediate future. Alternatives such as industry support, vouchers, and innovative bloc grant funding are perhaps the only avenues open to the child care profession to explore for improving the situation. In the meantime, we must work to improve society's over-all image of the child care worker. We must become outspoken advocates and educate the public to its responsibility to make child care and supportive services for families an integral part of community planning.

Keeping a Healthy Perspective on It All

The purpose of presenting the previous material was not to give you sweaty palms, a tense back, or blurred vision. Yes, burnout is a serious problem, but we don't want to let our awareness of the issue render us immobile. It is important that we be able to recognize when our circuits register an overload and distinguish the various stress factors in our lives, but increased awareness should not keep us from experiencing life fully. Rather, we should use our new knowledge to consciously develop personal strategies to prevent the signs of burnout from sliding irreversibly downward.

While this section focused on many of the negative aspects of the child care role, the picture is not one of total doom and gloom. An awareness of the burnout syndrome has already provided impetus for many child care workers to develop safety valves and restore a sense of balance in their lives. They have found it possible not only to handle the demands of their jobs and keep stress and burnout in check, but to reengineer their lives to keep stretching and growing.

The first and most fundamental prescription for success is realistic self-assessment. This will set the stage for subsequent sections of this book that apply the particulars of managing time, space and people to check and conquer burnout.

Part Two: RX FOR SUCCESS

Chapter 2
Self-Assessment

Taking The First Step

"Would you tell me, please
which way I ought to walk from here?"
"That depends a good deal
on where you want to get to," said the cat.
"I don't much care where,"
said Alice.
"Then it doesn't matter
which way you walk," said the cat.
"So long as I get somewhere,"
Alice added as an explanation.
"Oh, you're sure to do that,"
said the cat, "if you only walk long enough!"
Alice in Wonderland

Like Alice, some people amble through life without ever really assessing themselves or making explicit choices about personal and career opportunities. If you have managed to drift toward your destiny in this fashion without feeling the debilitating effects of stress and burnout, you are a fortunate individual. Many people find, however, such a haphazard method ultimately unsatisfying. Without deliberate direction, it is easy to slip into frustrating careers and get locked into unfulfilling lifestyles.

The secret to dealing with the future is first to define what we have to work with in the present. Then we can use these basic building blocks to construct a framework for making rational career decisions. Looking at the *here and now* means taking an honest inventory of our strengths, weaknesses, successes, and failures. Only in this way will we have clear pictures of ourselves and our needs, skills, talents, and preferences.

The first step is obviously not easy. Done properly, self-assessment takes time and may be uncomfortable. It is much easier to gloss over our flaws and idiosyncrasies than deal with them head on. But self-assessment is an essential step that shouldn't be rushed. Self-assessment lays the foundation for charting specific goals and helps maximize inner strengths and skills that in turn will harmonize our many roles. The process cannot be telescoped without risking erroneous judgments and misleading conclusions. It is a complex but necessary task, taking time, thought, and reflection.

For purposes of our analysis, we approach the self-assessment task from two directions. We look first at an individual's personal profile and then focus attention on his or her professional profile. Each area includes inventories and exercises that will aid in drawing up a composite profile—a balanced picture where both dimensions of an individual's life exist in harmony.

Who's in charge?

You will notice in this section the conspicuous absence of rating scales to interpret your responses. That is deliberate. If we put too much stock in analysis developed by someone else, we take out of our own hands the responsibility for interpreting, assessing, and understanding. It then becomes all too easy also to shift responsibility for change. No one can tell you what you can or cannot do with your life or how good a person you are. All others can do is supply potentially relevant information which you can then use to create a clearer picture of yourself and develop a strategy for decision making. But you must make sense out of the information. You have to do the analysis, and you are in charge. This is the essence of true self-assessment.[1]

By your actions through the day, the week and the year, you already know if you are achieving the kind of life you want for yourself and your family. You already know if your management of time, space, and people is "superior," "outstanding," "adequate," "needs improvement," "hopeless," or any shade in between. You don't need some arbitrary number rating to tell you that you feel tense, tired, and wiped out at the end of the day or that you should change certain habits to save yourself.

What is most important in the final analysis is how you perceive yourself and how you feel about what you are doing and achieving. To deny this makes it too easy to fall prey to someone else's interpretation of how you are and how you ought to feel.

Looking at Your Personal Profile

Only you know your strengths, limitations, skills, and talents. Your ability to see yourself as you really are requires that you have a clear picture of your merits as well as your shortcomings.

Physically, what kind of specimen are you? How do you rate your over-all health, stamina, and energy level? How do you feel about your physical appearance? What kind of priority does your health and appearance play in your life?

Intellectually, do you have a realistic understanding of your strengths and limitations? How would you assess your problem-solving skills, talent for writing, interest in reading, and ability to articulate? How is your attention span? Can you sit and listen to a long lecture or watch a four-hour epic movie without squirming, or do you identify with the three-year-olds at your center and like to move on to something new after a few minutes?

Socially, how would you assess your listening and communication skills? Do people choose you to unload their problems? How often do you find you turn to your close circle of friends for counsel and advice? Do you feel you are valued as a friend? By whom, and for what qualities?

Emotionally and spiritually, where do you stand? Do you consider yourself an optimist, realist, or a pessimist? How would you rate your general attitude on life, your over-all mood level and disposition? What are your needs for spiritual renewal and what value does this sense of security hold in your life?

Finally, do you think your friends, spouse, and work associates have an accurate perception of who you really are? It has been said that it is difficult to see the picture when you're inside the frame. If your friends filled out the following inventory, would their answers correspond to yours? If not, would you want to correct the misperceptions?

Exercise 1
Tapping my resources—where do I stand?

Jot down your personal resources in the following categories. Don't be modest! If you don't toot your own horn, who will? Likewise, don't be afraid to unearth those idiosyncrasies that may need some improving. Realistic self-assessment must begin with looking at both our positive and negative attributes.

- *Physical resources:*

- *Intellectual resources:*

- *Social resources:*

- *Emotional and spiritual resources:*

Exercise 2
What traits describe me?

Check on the continuum where you think you fit in each of the following areas.

- I enjoy working on a team   __/__/__/__/__   I prefer to work alone

- I have a high energy level and like a fast pace   __/__/__/__/__   I enjoy a relaxed, casual pace in my work

- I like a lot of structure and organization in work   __/__/__/__/__   I prefer an informal, loose working environment

- I prefer a change in routine regularly   __/__/__/__/__   I enjoy repetitive tasks and little change in routine

- I am open to constructive criticism of my efforts   __/__/__/__/__   I feel uneasy and sometimes defensive when critiqued

- I like challenges, even at the risk of failure   __/__/__/__/__   I prefer to play it safe. I like a margin of safety

- I like to work with data, figures, and computations   __/__/__/__/__   I do not like to work with analytical data and computations

- I like to be in the spotlight   __/__/__/__/__   I like to work behind the scenes

- I enjoy large social gatherings and meeting people   __/__/__/__/__   I prefer small intimate social gatherings with old friends

- I will not hesitate to return an item to a store if it isn't just right   __/__/__/__/__   If I've made a mistake buying something, I'll keep it rather than return it

- I will ask people to lower their voices if they are bothersome in a theatre   __/__/__/__/__   I prefer non-confrontation and will move to another seat

Exercise 3
My "scrimp" and "splurge" indicators

Our checkbook can often provide clues as to what we value in our lives. Since we all make decisions about where our limited dollars are spent, our priorities are usually reflected in those decisions. Take a few minutes to look at the list below. Put a minus sign next to those categories that you tend to "scrimp" on and a plus sign next to those that you like to "splurge" on.

_____ Home furnishings

_____ Food (eaten at home)

_____ Dining out in restaurants

_____ Clothing

_____ Car

_____ Beauty needs

_____ Recreation, fitness, sports, health clubs

_____ Entertainment (shows, theatre, etc.)

_____ Liquor

_____ Telephone

_____ Utilities (like air conditioning)

_____ Gifts for others

_____ Vacations and travel

_____ Medicine and health care

_____ Books, magazines

_____ Donations to church and charities

_____ Housecleaning or maintenance

_____ Stereo and records

_____ Little extras, self indulgences

_____ Other:

Exercise 4
A look at my accomplishments

It is easy to look at life through cloudy glasses, particularly if we feel we are not living up to our expectations. But how often do we balance the picture by looking at all the things that we have accomplished and achieved? Take a few minutes now to dwell on five accomplishments you have had in the past year in your personal life apart from your job or professional life. They need not be earthshaking, but just five things in which you felt a sense of pride.

1.

2.

3.

4.

5.

Now go back and ask yourself the following questions: Were these accomplishments important because they were something you achieved for yourself, that you did for someone else, or that straddled both categories?

Exercise 5
A satisfying task

Any role is a flexible combination of tasks that can be arranged or rearranged in varying ways. If we isolate the elements that truly give us enjoyment, we can structure our future activities to correspond with those elements so that they, too, can be more pleasurable.

Think back to the last practical concrete project you did at home that you enjoyed doing immensely. Now try to isolate the specific parts of that task that gave you pleasure. For instance, if you prepared a fancy dinner for ten people, you may have enjoyed the experience because you had a babysitter for your children, worked alone, arranged flowers from your garden, tried a new recipe, had the music blaring while you prepared the meal, and basked in the appreciation of your friends at the end of the meal.

Your turn:

The biological factor

An integral part of self-assessment is understanding our own biological tempo and how that shapes our attitudes and perceptions of life.[2] For our internal clocks play a powerful role in mood fluctuations and energy and performance levels. These rhythms are naturally recurring cycles of biological activities governed by the nervous and hormonal systems. Some are completely internal. Others, it appears, are controlled by external stimulation such as exposure to light, heat, and changes in gravity, electromagnetic fields, barometric pressure, and cosmic rays. Biological rhythms can be viewed as survival mechanisms—natural fluctuations in the body processes which automatically dictate that periods of high energy be interspersed with periods of restorative inactivity.

We all have ample evidence in our own lives of patterns that indicate our inner rhythms. We experience times when we are "just not up to it," or when we feel particularly edgy. How often do we hear ourselves say that we're "having a bad day" or that we "got up on the wrong side of the bed"? Our awareness also extends beyond our personal sphere. For instance, child care workers know there are days when the children seem particularly wound up and more difficult to manage. They may hypothesize that such days even correspond to how gustily the wind is blowing or whether or not there is a full moon.

There are hundreds of other examples of rhythms and repeating cycles around us in the world of nature. How is it, for instance, that plants know when it is time to develop new buds, and certain animals instinctively know it is time to grow their winter coat or stash away food? Birds sense when to fly South to warmer locations and fish know when to swim upstream to spawn. The mystery of these powerful rhythms has fascinated scientists for years. But research is still inconclusive in determining the degree to which these are exogenous rhythms—influenced by external factors—or endogenous rhythms, controlled by internal regulators and independent on outside forces.

We have enough information now, however, regarding the health-related aspects of biological rhythms to understand that they may hold the answers to many mood and behavioral fluctua-

tion, as well as changes in immunity and incidence of illness, variations in toxicity of drugs, changes in body weight, appetite, motivation, energy levels, sexual interest, susceptibility to stress, and the occurrence of psychosomatic diseases. Research has identified three types of rhythms that influence virtually every measure of our psychological and physiological well-being.

The first of these, the one that most individuals are familiar with, is the *circadian rhythm* or 24-hour cycle. Our circadian cycle influences sleep, body temperature, and body functions such as blood pressure, pulse, respiration, blood sugar levels, amino acid levels, and ability to metabolize drugs. The changing levels of crucial hormones in our blood and the variations in concentration of essential brain chemicals also means there is a subtle rhythm to the efficiency with which we metabolize food, the quickness of our reaction time, and the keenness of our perception and discrimination skills. Virtually every aspect of human biology is influenced by this daily rhythm.

Ultradian rhythms are rhythms that occur in periods shorter than a day. Most current research is concentrating on the 90-minute rest/activity cycle that appear to influence appetite, attention span, and certain sleep patterns.

The third cyclic variation is known as *infradian rhythms.* These are rhythms that are longer than 24 hours, and that may last for days, weeks, or even months. These cycles are particularly tied to fluctuations in emotional responses, as well as changes in motivation, hunger, and performance levels. There is speculation that infradian cycles may also influence periodic fluctuations in weight, appetite, ability to sleep, and creativity level. The popular notion of charting infradian rhythms, commonly referred to as biorhythms, was developed from the research of Wilhelm Fliess who published his formula for the use of biological rhythms in 1887. His basic theory has been expanded and currently focuses on three infradian variations: a 23-day physical cycle, a 28-day emotional cycle, and a 33-day intellectual cycle. These presumably begin the day we are born and continue throughout our lives in a regular pattern.

While we may question the validity of individual theories, we can glean insights from the research that will help us understand the ebb and flow of our own rhythms throughout the day, week, or month. For we each have our own way of experiencing time, our own framework that shapes our attitudes, perceptions, and feelings regarding time. We can learn to use that time frame as a tool for understanding ourselves and our own unique biological rhythm.

Since every individual has a unique tempo and biological rhythm profile, record keeping (physical or mental) is the only way to plot the subtleties that may make a difference in mood, energy level, and behavior in general. If nothing else, the activity puts us in touch with our rhythms and our environment, and may even strongly influence our attitudes and behavior. Knowledge of the influences of rhythms in our lives can eliminate the tension of uncertainty by explaining, and perhaps even predicting, fluctuations. This can reduce the self-doubt that often accompanies normal variations in behavior and performance.

Exercise 6
Am I in step?

To get an accurate reading of your biological rhythms, it is necessary to look at fluctuations over an extended period of time, preferably 30 days or longer. So the commitment you make to this exercise is different than the other quick assessments in this book. The inventory is easy to fill out, however, and should take only a few minutes each time you do it.

You'll need roughly 25 copies of the inventory form, since you'll be doing the exercises on five different days during a 30-day period and five times on each of those days. On Day One, fill out the form at roughly 4-hour intervals throughout your waking hours (for example: 7 a.m., 11 a.m., 3 p.m., 7 p.m., 11 p.m.). The exact times are not important. What is important is that you allow some interval of time between each assessment and are consistent on each of the five days. When you have completed the five forms for Day One, clip these together and indicate the date. Also make a note of whether you felt the day was fairly typical or if some unusual circumstances (friends visiting, pressures at work, your cat died, etc.) may have influenced how you felt.

Wait five days and repeat the series. Wait another five days and do the exercise again. By the time the 30 days are over, you will have completed all 25 forms and your targeted dates throughout the month will have included both weekdays and weekends.

When you have completed your survey, spread out the forms and tally your results, noting fluctuations and consistent patterns. What insights can you draw from this information? Are there regular times during the day when your hearing is most sensitive? When you feel most peppy and alert? When your mental concentration is at its peak? Don't get carried away in your self-analysis, but your new awareness should be helpful in planning your daily activities so that they are in harmony with your rhythms.

Biological Rhythms Inventory

Date _____   Time _____

Note on the continuum provided how you presently feel in the following areas:

- *Mental concentration*

  alert
  and attentive   __/__/__/__/__   day dreaming, distracted

- *Appetite*

  famished,
  starving   __/__/__/__/__   full and satisfied

- *General energy level*

  peppy,
  rarin' to go   __/__/__/__/__   sluggish, tired

- *Overall mood*

  exhilarated,
  happy   __/__/__/__/__   depressed, feeling low

- *General stress level*

  tense
  and anxious   __/__/__/__/__   tranquil and relaxed

- *Sociability*

  talkative,
  outgoing   __/__/__/__/__   quiet, withdrawn

- *Sensitivity to noise*

  play
  the drums   __/__/__/__/__   a pin dropping is TOO loud

- *Sensitivity to heat*

  chilled
  and shivering   __/__/__/__/__   hot and sweating

- *Sensitivity to light*

  put on
  the spotlight   __/__/__/__/__   squinting, eyes tearing

What are you presently doing or about to do?_____
Any physical symptoms evident? (headache, stiffness, digestive difficulties, etc.)

Weight: normal ____ under ____ over ____
Any unusual circumstances affecting present behavior and feelings?

Exercise 7
My sleeping/waking patterns

"If we sleep one half hour less per day,
this would correspond over a lifetime to a
total of two years."   **Godfrey Lebhar**

It is told that the eccentric Salvador Dali would sit on a chair with a tin plate positioned at his feet. He would then dangle a spoon loosely between his fingers, close his eyes, and fall into a deep sleep. The spoon would fall and the clatter of metal would jolt him awake. Dali claimed that he would be completely refreshed by the amount of sleep he got from the brief interval it took the spoon to fall.[3] Bizarre indeed, but others in history, notably Churchill, Edison, Gladstone, and Napoleon, all had unusual sleeping patterns, often replenishing themselves by quick catnaps throughout the day.

How about you? Are you a night owl or a morning monkey? Take a few minutes to answer the questions below to gain insights into your own sleeping/waking patterns.

• Do you have difficulty falling asleep or staying asleep?

• Do you need an alarm clock to wake up in the morning? How loud?

• Are your waking patterns different on weekends or vacations?

• How would you describe your morning routine? Do you jump out of bed eagerly or take all morning to wake up gradually?

• Do you nap regularly?

• Do your sleep patterns follow a consistent routine (asleep every night at nearly the same time and awake at roughly the same time each morning)?

• Do you have any bedtime rituals?

• Have you noticed any correlation between what you eat in the evening (and when) and how well you sleep?

• Do you feel you get enough sleep most nights?

Looking at Your Professional Profile

Perhaps the most important strategy for preventing job burn-out is to recognize just what aspects of our professional lives contribute to excessive stress. It is also important to assess what aspects of work give satisfaction and promote feelings of accomplishment. Only in this way will we be able to tailor the position to be stimulating and challenging, and one to which we will want to make a long-term commitment.

While administrators and teachers differ in how they perceive their roles and the problems associated with them, most of the following exercises are applicable to either type of position. Where the questions are more appropriate for one or the other, however, this has been indicated at the top of the inventory.

Exercise 8
How did I get here anyway?

The inquiring reporter asked the young woman
why she wanted to be a mortician. "Because,"
she said, "I enjoy working with people."

The San Francisco Chronicle[1]

People who enter early childhood education are usually idealistic and eager to improve conditions for young children. Often, though, they lack insight into their motivations for entering the field and end up disillusioned when expectations don't match reality.

A logical starting point, then, for compiling our professional profile is to take a trip back in time to assess just how it was that we were steered in the direction of early childhood education in the first place.

• Can you pinpoint two events (or individuals) in your life that you consider instrumental in your decision to take your present position?

• Describe what you perceived your role would be at that time.

• Was your initial impression and understanding of your role correct?

• Was your training adequate to prepare you for what the position entails?

• Do you consider your work a job or a career?

• Would you choose child care work again if you could retrace your steps and make new decisions about your education and career prospects?

• Do you still get a feeling of satisfaction and sense of accomplishment from your work, or is it less interesting now than it used to be?

Exercise 9
How do I evaluate my work situation?

Many times job satisfaction boils down to simply adding up the pluses and the minuses. While this in no way tells the whole story, it does give clues to potential trouble spots.

Before each aspect of your job, indicate with plus or minus sign whether or not it has contributed to or subtracted from your over-all job satisfaction. If the item has not had an influence one way or another, leave it blank.

_____ Salary and benefits

_____ Flexibility in hours

_____ Opportunities for advancement

_____ Enhanced prestige

_____ Companionship with co-workers

_____ Relationship with parents of students

_____ Chance to use talents and skills

_____ Time for leisure activities

_____ Time to pursue educational goals

_____ Opportunities to grow and learn from colleagues

_____ A feeling of independence

_____ Vacation, leave schedule

_____ Overall self-respect

Exercise 10
My satisfaction curve

Sometimes visuals capture the essence of our feelings far better than words. If you had to plot your satisfaction profile on a graph that would illustrate your over-all attitude toward your work during the time you have held your position, what shape would your satisfaction curve take?

The horizontal indicator assesses time on the job. These marks may signify months or years, depending on your own situation. The vertical indicator assesses over-all attitude and enthusiasm level, low beginning at the juncture and high moving upward.

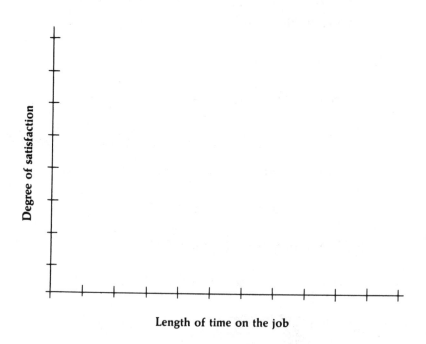

Length of time on the job

After you have drawn your curve, take a second look and ask yourself what events, incidents, or people were instrumental at different points along the bottom line that influenced the degree of satisfaction you experienced on the job at that particular time.

Exercise 11
A look at my accomplishments on the job

*"In our haste to deal with the things that are wrong,
let us not upset the things that are right."*

Just as we took the time in our personal profile to look at our positive accomplishments over the last year, let's take a look at the hurdles you have gotten over and the achievements you have made on your job as well. Again, they need not be monumental accomplishments, but things that gave you a feeling of success when you completed them.

1.

2.

3.

4.

5.

Exercise 12 (for classroom teachers)
How do I feel about my role?

	Always	Occa-sionally	Never

• Do you feel you get the recognition you deserve for your work from your head teacher or director? ____ ____ ____

• Do you feel your director understands your needs and interests, and makes good use of your talents and skills? ____ ____ ____

• Do you believe your fellow teachers feel you are doing a good job and assuming your share of the work load? ____ ____ ____

• Do you find that you want to take the day off for no other reason than you just don't feel like working? ____ ____ ____

• Do you ever contemplate quitting your job? ____ ____ ____

• Do you feel that if you quit tomorrow your position would be easily filled and the program not disrupted? ____ ____ ____

• Do you have difficulty controlling your students? ____ ____ ____

• Do you feel your work is supervised too closely? ____ ____ ____

• Do you believe your position makes good use of your training experience, and potential? ____ ____ ____

• Do you believe the parents of your students are doing a satisfactory job of teaching and caring for their children? ____ ____ ____

• Do you feel isolated, with no one to consult or talk to about your job frustrations? ____ ____ ____

• Do you look at the clock regularly during the day and fight to keep boredom from settling in? ____ ____ ____

Exercise 13 (for program administrators)
How well do I handle my multifaceted responsibilities?

The effective child care administrator must have the skills of both a task specialist and a human relations specialist. This means balancing the needs of the organization to run efficiently (budgets, maintenance, planning, etc.) while still meeting the needs of the people who work at the center (guiding, motivating, counseling, modeling). It is a rare person, indeed, who can juggle the many responsibilities and still maintain a sense of equilibrium. Many directors are more proficient in one set of skills than the other and as a consequence see part of their program suffer.

Following is a list of twenty activities comprising qualities from both areas of center administration. Put a check next to ten of these items that represent how you spend a typical day at your school.

_____ 1. Giving a tour of the center to prospective parents of new students.

_____ 2. Organizing curriculum materials for a study unit (science, math, art, reading).

_____ 3. Interviewing a potential teacher's aide.

_____ 4. Listening to a parent talk about her difficulties with child rearing.

_____ 5. Planning menus for snack or lunch for the upcoming month.

_____ 6. Meeting with two teachers to help resolve a conflict over overlapping duties.

_____ 7. Previewing and cataloging new curriculum books for the staff library.

_____ 8. Preparing a new tuition schedule for the following year.

_____ 9. Conducting a brainstorming staff meeting on ways to reduce spending.

_____ 10. Writing and designing a new brochure for the center.

_____ 11. Filling out the quarterly tax statement for the IRS.

_____ 12. Helping a teacher draw up a list of field trip possibilities for the month.

_____ 13. Preparing a financial statement for a board of directors meeting.

_____ 14. Ordering art and office supplies from the local supplier.

_____ 15. Making some new musical instruments for the classroom.

_____ 16. Demonstrating how to conduct a "circle time" activity to a new teacher.

_____ 17. Meeting with a teacher to discuss ways to handle a disruptive student.

_____ 18. Fixing a leaking faucet in the kitchen sink.

_____ 19. Talking to a group of high school students about career opportunities in child care.

_____ 20. Conducting an orientation session for a group of new volunteers.

Now go through this list of activities a second time. Select ten items that you would prefer to spend your time doing if you knew that all the other areas would be covered adequately by someone else. Rank-order these items from 1 (most prefer) to 10 (least prefer).

Next go over each of your lists. Check to see if either of your ratings are lopsided in the way you are currently spending your time or in the way you would prefer to spend your time. (The following activities would generally fall within the category of the task specialist: 2, 5, 7, 8, 10, 11, 13, 14, 15, and 18. All remaining activities would generally fall in the category of human-relations specialist.)

Do you feel that the balance (or imbalance) of your responses indicates that your over-all performance on the job might be affected adversely?

The Personal-Professional Tug-of-War

Our lives are an intricate web of relationships connecting our personal and professional worlds. Job, family, friends, and outside commitments all make demands on our time and energy and are inextricably related in the way they affect our performance both on and off the job. It sounds like a grand conspiracy, doesn't it? We are caught in the middle with all our allegiances and loyalties tugged from every direction.

Web of relationships

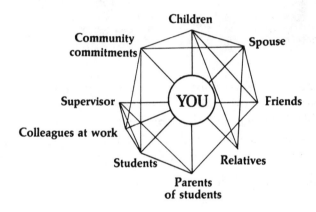

Much of the frustration and stress that child care workers experience is the result of trying to fulfill all those commitments with unrealistically rigid expectations. They view their professional and personal commitments separately and try to be a model of perfection in each role.[5] Pursuing this strategy of separation can only be harmful to one's mental health.

Looking at the *total* picture of commitments makes far more sense, freeing us to think in terms of more realistic expectations. This allows us to acknowledge that there will be many times when

our personal and professional commitments compete for our attention; that our work *will* interfere with family life; and that juggling of priorities *will* be absolutely necessary. Balancing conflicting demands means trading off time and energy in one area today for time and energy in another tomorrow or next week.

Embracing this philosophy and putting it into practice are quite different things, however. Trying to balance the conflicting commitments in our professional and personal lives means that some of the people involved in our web of relationships will feel shortchanged. We must keep reminding ourselves that loyalty to either part does not mean slavery.[6] It is possible to be faithful to an organization, devoting ourselves with honesty and integrity, without becoming its servant.

In fact, some would argue, a certain amount of detachment from our professional role may be essential to maintaining a healthy perspective. Detachment is not the same as indifference. People enter the child care field because they care about other people. But they will continue to expend energy doing things that benefit others only if they feel they are receiving reciprocal benefits, and that their own mental health needs are met.

Survival in a profession that demands so much psychic energy depends on our being able to negotiate between our many roles, accept our limitations, and help others appreciate the total scope of our commitments. At first this may mean that we have to make a conscious effort to share openly with our colleagues, family, and friends just how our juggling act affects them. But the payoff is worth it. As their appreciation of our situation increases, the groundwork will be established for ongoing support to help us maintain that sense of harmony and balance between our personal and professional worlds.

The subtle distinction between role and style

In our personal and professional worlds we take on a number of different roles. We may be a daughter or son, a wife or husband, a mother or father, or a teacher or director. Each role brings with it a host of expectations for behavior. How we perceive that role at times may be quite different from how others perceive it, but in any case it serves to describe the duties, responsibilities, and standard activities we associate with it.

These broad role categories say nothing, however, about *how* we carry out the responsibilities or each role. The role of teacher, for instance, assumes the general functions of instructing children, working with parents, preparing the learning environment, etc. But the ways of implementing those functions may range from warm and sensitive to cold and authoritarian.[7] This is the distinction between *role* and *style*. The term style describes *how* we carry out the activities associated with any role.

We tend to put so much emphasis on the roles we play that we neglect to assess just what style we're striving for. We move through adulthood with the assumption that it is our accomplishments, titles, and roles that are most important; yet it is often our style that people remember. The people we associate with usually remember us by how we treated them. If our style was thoughtful, patient, sharing, giving, we will be remembered long and well.

Exercise 14
What roles do I play?

At home I am:	People who depend on me	For what purpose:
_____	_____	_____
_____	_____	_____
_____	_____	_____
_____	_____	_____
	_____	_____
	_____	_____
		_____

At work: I am:

_____	_____	_____
_____	_____	_____
_____	_____	_____
_____	_____	_____
	_____	_____
	_____	_____

Exercise 15
My style

From the list below, select ten words that you feel convey how you relate to people at home and at work. Don't hesitate to add any others that you can think of.

reflective	dependable
assertive	demanding
warm	cautious
sensitive	thoughtful
articulate	patient
polite	short-tempered
fast-paced	humorous
plodding	punctual
methodical	competitive
kind	shy
quiet	impatient

at home: at work:

_____   _____

_____   _____

_____   _____

_____   _____

_____   _____

_____   _____

Now think of a good friend or a person you particularly admire. What words describe his/her style?

_____   _____   _____   _____

Postscript on Self-Assessment— Accepting the Givens

"God, grant me the serenity to accept the things I cannot change,
The courage to change the things I can,
And the wisdom to know the difference."

The everyday demands upon our personal and professional lives make it increasingly difficult to escape the adverse effects of stress. It is difficult if not impossible to maintain our equilibrium if we focus our energies on trying to change the impossible, whatever it may be—our daily commute, inflation, city noise and fumes, bureaucratic red tape. We can't think about changing the world without getting a global headache. So an integral part of self-assessment is to develop a realistic framework for sorting out potential frustrations in our lives and how we will confront them.

"Accepting the givens" holds that it is not only valid but healthy to recognize that some problems inherent in our society, our profession, or our work environment are beyond our control *for the time being.* That is not the same as saying that we should resign ourselves to certain injustices forever. It does mean that for the present we must focus our energies where they will do the *most* good, accepting what we cannot change and changing what we can.

Exercise 16
My roadblocks

List ten things that frustrate you about your work environment or your personal life, things that stand in your way and act as roadblocks in your performance. If you're stuck as to where to begin, think back to this past week. Recall the things you complained about to your colleagues, friends, or family, or kept quietly to yourself.

Next to each item, indicate whether or not this source of frustration fits into the realm of things that you have the power to change, or things that you are powerless to change within the foreseeable future.

	Things I can change	Things I must accept for the time being
1.	____	____
2.	____	____
3.	____	____
4.	____	____
5.	____	____
6.	____	____
7.	____	____
8.	____	____
9.	____	____
10.	____	____

Chapter 3
Managing Time

The Nature of Time—An Overview

Ever since man observed the first dawn creep over the horizon, he has wrestled with the mysteries of time and the inexplicable nature of its daily cycle. Time is the raw material of life

weaving its way through every aspect of our daily existence. Befuddled by its abstract elusiveness, we have calculated, analyzed, and scrutinized time in our attempt to gain a greater appreciation of its powerful permutations. We can waste time, lose time, pass the time away, and even march along with time, but we'll never be able to beat it or bottle it. In the end, time is always victorious, dominating the rhythms of our universe.

We take for granted our use of the hour and day as a convenient way of measuring time. But our clock is only an artificial measuring device that defines our concept of the passage of time. One hour equals one-twenty-fourth of the duration of the earth's complete rotation on its axis. The words that we associate with time are merely useful conventions in our own "time language."[1] To the extent, though, that we can understand its potent influence in our own behavior, we can shape our use of time, to work within its boundaries and maximize its potential in our lives. Time

management recognizes that time is indeed a precious commodity, one that can't be overlooked in our effort to lead a rich, fulfilling, and productive live.

In many ways the term "time management" is a misnomer. We can't manage the clock. We can't accumulate time, save it, or store it, and once spent, we can't retrieve it. All we can do is manage ourselves to utilize time more efficiently. The wonderful thing about time, though, is that it is equitably distributed to all. We all have the same amount of time. We all must live within the confines of 168 hours each week whether we are rich or poor, a child care worker, a doctor, or a musician. So our problem is not a lack of time—we have all there is—but rather what we do with the time we have.

Since time waits for no one, we have to take the initiative. We have to deliberately apply management techniques to stretch our allocation of time and create a time cushion in our lives. But we only have so many options. We can either reduce the amount of time we spend on an activity, or we can structure the environment to reduce the time demands placed on us. Put another way, we have to tap our resources and apply every creative short cut and gimmick to do *fewer* things, do what we can *faster*, and do them more *efficiently*.

Time Management—working smarter, not harder

Some people are dedicated to the notion that hard work alone is the measure of importance. Success is equated with sheer output of energy. But there is not always a direct correlation between hard work and quality of results. Moreover, people who focus their lives on long, hard hours of work may fall easy prey to Parkinson's Law which cautions that "Any task will expand to the amount of time allocated to it." When such people apply time management techniques, they tend to fill up their newly found time with more hard work.

The ultimate goal of time management should not be to enable us to do more work in the extra time, but rather to do other personally satisfying things. This orientation puts a qualitative element into the equation. We should be striving to work *smarter*, not *harder*.

In this section we shall apply many techniques that will help us manage our time (and our lives) more effectively. The process is logical and methodical, following a course of "common sense." It includes: 1) charting goals for the future that are realistic and achievable; 2) planning for priorities to maximize effectiveness; 3) learning to schedule time productively; and 4) clearing hurdles like procrastination and interruptions.

Before we can plan the judicious use of our time tomorrow, however, we need to assess the impact of time in our lives today. Only careful assessment of our attitudes and behavior patterns will provide clues that will make time management meaningful for our own unique set of circumstances. Time use is too personal to glean from books alone all the information we need to exercise control. Our personal habits and patterns must be the real source of insight.

Exercises 17 and 18 will help us look at our own perception of time and the role it plays in our life. Some people, for instance, are far more "time sensitive" than others.[2] They are constantly "tuned in" to the pressures of time and aware of its influence on their every move. Others are more casual, even oblivious, to its influence and only vaguely aware how they respond to it.

Exercise 19 is designed to help us assess how we are currently using time on a day-to-day basis. Many of us give little thought to where our time actually goes. We might sense that it is slipping away and beyond our control, but asked to estimate how we think we spend our time and then actually documenting where it went, we are surprised, often shocked, at the time-robbers that have gobbled up our day.

To improve our time management skills, we have to allocate a little extra time at the outset to determine the direction we want to go. "Making time" may take a disproportionate amount of time at first, but the investment of time at this stage will pay off in future dividends.

Exercise 17
How time-sensitive am I?

	Always	Occa-sionally	Never

• I feel that I must always be busy doing something productive and am somewhat guilty if I just relax and loaf. ___ ___ ___

• Whenever possible, I try to do more than one thing at a time like exercise while I watch television, or eat while I drive. ___ ___ ___

• I get annoyed when someone shows up late for an appointment and keeps me waiting. ___ ___ ___

• I am lost without my watch or a clock close at hand. ___ ___ ___

• I get quite impatient if I have to wait in a line at the bank or grocery store. ___ ___ ___

• Slow drivers perturb me. ___ ___ ___

• I find myself completing the sentences of others in an effort to move the conversation along. ___ ___ ___

Exercise 18
How well do I manage my time?

	Always	Occa-sionally	Never

• I tend to underestimate how much time a particular project or task will take.

• I regularly work long hours, yet I still take work home with me in the evenings and weekends.

• I tend to procrastinate for so long that unpleasant tasks become panic situations.

• I seem to be beseiged during the day with interruptions that prevent me from doing my job.

• I wonder why I subscribe to newspapers, journals, and magazines since they're usually out of date by the time I get around to reading them.

• I have a jogging suit (or tennis racquet, etc.) I got last Christmas that still has the price tag on it.

• Birthdays, anniversaries, and other occasions seem to slip my mind.

• I arrive at appointments out of breath (or not at all).

• I seem to get part way into a task and find that I have to stop before I finish it.

• I find myself driving too fast, eating too fast, and in a constant battle with the clock.

Exercise 19
My time log

Select what you feel will be a fairly typical day at work, one that includes the full range of activities that are part of your role. Begin your time log when you first wake up in the morning and make notations every 20 minutes throughout the day. Admittedly this is time consuming but once you get into the swing of it, your actual writing time will be minimal. Indicate the time, the activity, and your general feelings and attitude at that moment. Since memories can be notoriously fuzzy, it is important that you not rely on your memory to fill in the blanks later on. This log is not intended to be a part of your regular routine. Rather, it is a diagnostic tool that you can use to assess how well you are presently managing your time. You might also want to fill out another time log on a typical weekend day.

Be honest with yourself. This time log is for you and you alone. You won't benefit from the experience if you only record what you think you should be doing or thinking. If your quick telephone call lapsed into 20 minutes, record it.

When you have completed the exercise, relive your day with the following questions in mind, which will help you understand your work patterns:

• What determined the order of things that you worked on today? Did you do the easy things before the more difficult? Did you follow the squeaky wheel principle and attend to the "loudest" things first? Or did you do the things that required a small amount of time before doing the things that required a lot of time?

• Did you finish what you had to do on an activity or project before starting something new, or was your day characterized by jumping from one task to another?

• Why did you do the activities at the time you did them? Was this by your own choice, because of demands placed on you by others, or because you just "fell" into them at that particular time? Did you stick to tasks that you found interesting and avoid the less interesting?

Time Log

Date _____

Time	Activity	Feelings

Time	Activity	Feelings

Charting Goals for the Future

*"The direction you are facing has a lot to
do with your destination."*

Formulating a goals statement is in many ways like taking an instant snapshot and watching the image develop before our eyes. Deliberately commiting to paper what we want out of life brings our future into view and gives us an image of the direction we're heading. A realistic goals statement puts our unique stamp on the future and gives purpose to our actions. It embodies our very philosophy of life by reflecting the things that are important to us.

Defining goals is not an exercise in clairvoyance, though. Quite the contrary. It means taking the time to reflect upon our present and future needs and how we hope to achieve them. Our goals can then serve as signposts to guide us through life, preventing us from embarking upon a course of action where mere activity replaces well-monitored progress.

If logic and common sense tell us that well-formulated goals are essential for achieving fulfillment in life, why then is taking the time to draw up goals anathema to most people? Perhaps it is because we have been conditioned to think of goals as great lifetime aspirations such as, "I want to be happy," "I want to be successful," or "I want to achieve my full potential." Such goals seem so overwhelming and abstract that they defy a rational plan of action. So in frustration we rationalize, "Oh well, I've got my whole lifetime to achieve happiness (success, my potential, etc.) so there is certainly no rush to get started *today!*"

But our goals need not remain intellectual abstractions. There are ways to make our goals more purposeful and achievable. The key is twofold: goals must be realistic and they must be manageable.

There is an enormous difference between vague dreams or wishful thinking and clear, well-conceived goals. *Realistic goals* are precisely defined and achievable. Reaching for the moon may be fine for astronauts, but we should set our sights closer to familiar ground. Setting realistic goals means looking at the resources, skills, talents, and preferences we highlighted in the self-assessment exercises and putting them into a workable, achievable time frame. It also means continually assessing and reassessing the "givens" in any situation so that our goals stay within the realistic realm of what we can hope to accomplish. Exercise 20 entails designing a perfect day—idealized but achievable because it builds on what we already have.

Manageable goals means pinpointing specific steps that work toward measurable and achievable ends. Some of the goals we echoed in the past were probably not very helpful because they did not tell us how we were to accomplish them. We cannot *do* a goal in the same way that we balance a checkbook or drive a car. All we can do is a series of things which when completed will demonstrate that the goal has been reached. But our goals statements will forever remain fuzzy unless we isolate those specific steps and define concrete, measurable tasks that we can act upon and evaluate.

To reduce stress and the causes of burnout in our lives, it is incumbent on us to translate our abstract goals into well-defined performance tasks that make goals behavioral, achievable, and able to be acted upon and evaluated. Only in this way will we have a real sense of accomplishment for all our hard work. Exercise 21 is a goals blueprint that will aid in this task of formulating manageable goals.

Exercise 20
Designing a perfect day

It has been said that life is a series of single days. To live a full, satisfying life, we must first begin to live full, satisfying days.[3] We strive for the ideal but sometimes don't stop to assess what that "ideal" means to us personally. Think back to your most recent truly satisfying day when your personal and professional lives really seemed compatible, when everything clicked just right.

Now try to pinpoint why that day went so well. Isolate all the particulars, the small incidental things that contributed to that great feeling. Think in terms of seemingly unimportant factors, too, like the weather, the amount of sleep you had, what you ate for breakfast, your pace, planning, and order of events during the day if you feel they helped contribute to that "perfect" atmosphere.

If you could design a perfect day for yourself three years from now, what would it be like? Not a complete fantasy day, but one that takes into account the skills and talents you have already acquired and those you feel you can acquire in the next three years.

In drawing up the particulars, think about your idealized self-image. What kind of person would you like to be? Including elements of your personal and professional worlds, write a detailed description of that person including role responsibilities, style, skills, and personal traits as well as the over-all environments of work and home. This exercise is important because, to a large extent, striving for balance in our lives is how we create a more positive identity. If we just act the way we'd like to be, we often find that we become the way we act.

Obviously, there is no one right way to complete this exercise. The exact nature of your perfect day is not as important as your ability to define in simple, direct language the characteristics that are important to you. Writing them down takes them out of the realm of vague, utopian dreams. It solidifies them in your mind and gives you something concrete to begin working toward.

Your turn:

Exercise 21
My goals blueprint

The following goals blueprint[4] is your guide for developing a step-by-step strategy for achieving goals. From completing the previous self-assessment exercises, you probably have a clear idea now of your "needs"—those things you want to change or accomplish. The business of developing goals begins with an examination of those needs, looking at them in relation to the resources you have. In doing this exercise, think of the zoom lens on a 35mm camera. The wide angle perspective takes in your broad goals. As you narrow the range of view, the subgoals, activities, and resources needed to carry out those goals come into sharp focus.

Let's begin:

1. In the column labeled **Goal**, select one broad goal that you would like to target in the next one to three years. This goal becomes the qualitative description of your desired ends. In other words, it states the broad result that you hope to achieve. It should be general in nature and include words like: *more, better, increased, diminished, improved.* Standing alone it may look like a glittering generality. But by the time you have completed all the steps in your goals blueprint, this broad goal will seem far more achievable.

2. The second category of **Subgoals** is the real heart of our blueprint because it provides the quantitative description of the goal we are striving toward. It should include information about *who, what, for how many, and by when.* These can be stated in a phrase that begins with the word "to." This descriptive phrase should also say something about the standards you need to achieve your goals. This is difficult because words like "to know," "to understand," "to appreciate" are all subjective. Sometimes it helps to set up a comparative standard such as "to perform better than . . ." or establish criteria that limit and define standards such as "to write . . ." or "to list . . . ." The key to developing good subgoals is to set standards that are challenging but not so difficult as to be impossible.

3. In the third column titled **Activities**, list every possible activity that will be necessary to accomplish each of the subgoals.

Try to put these activities in the order of when they should be done. You may have ten or more activities for each subgoal.

4. Time. How long do you project the activity will take? This category, like the others, may need to be adjusted as your goals move from formulation to implementation. Once you actually get going on the designated activities, your approximate time will become more accurate and you may need to revise them accordingly.

5. The category of **Resources Needed** is divided into three subcategories: the person or persons responsible for implementing the activity; materials and supplies necessary to complete it; and the approximate cost. In this planning stage, the figures might be rough estimates but at least they give some basis to decide if our goals and subgoals are achievable in light of our financial resources.

6. Checkpoints for Evaluation let you know if you are accomplishing your objectives. They may be actual products if your objective is to produce something tangible, or they may be points in time where you will assess your progress. This last category is important because you will be able to assess whether you did what you said you were going to or fell short of your stated goal. Evaluation also indicates the criteria that you will use to determine whether or not you met your goals. The more precise these are, the easier it will be for you to determine results.

In drawing up this goals blueprint, the goals you pursue must be your *own* goals and not those that you feel you ought to be striving for to please your family, friends, or colleagues. You are far more likely to work hard to accomplish goals that you have set for yourself and that you believe in. So make sure your goals come from your own needs and beliefs.

Filling out this goals blueprint does not mean that your goals become engraved in stone. Goals are not lifetime directives. In fact, the wonderful thing about goals is that they are *not* inflexible or static. As your needs, resources, and circumstances change, so too should your goals. Regular reevaluation, reassessing, and redefining your short and long-term goals is a healthy sign of growth in your professional and personal life.

"No wind favors he who has no destined port." **Montaigne**

MY GOALS BLUEPRINT

Goal	Subgoals	Action Steps	Time Needed	Resources Needed			Evaluation Checkpoints
				People	Materials	$$	
improved parent relations	- increase communication with each family this year by: • distributing monthly newsletter • sending home weekly "happy gram" progress notes	- select printer, get estimates for newsletter - collect ideas to include, schedule typist. Design format. - post schedule for happy grams to be sent	2 weeks ongoing 2 days	typist 3 hrs/mo. w/ teachers	printing services	$30/mo.	monthly weekly checklist
	- improve evaluation + feedback opportunities for parents by: • distributing feedback form in December + May • scheduling 2 parent conferences during year	- Write new evaluation feedback form. - Post conference schedule, send out confirmation notes to parents. - Schedule skills inventory for each child before conference.	1/2 days Nov. w/ staff 1/2 day 1/2 hr. per week with child		printing	$10	forms returned conference notes sent out in Oct. and Feb.
	- improve accessibility to parents by: • setting aside specific blocks of parent time each week where they can drop in • hosting an open house for all families in Sept. and May	- Announce "parent time" in newsletter. Post on bulletin board. - Select coordinate to help coordinate open house. - Arrange maintenance, food, publicity. - Prepare slide presentation about program.	2 days August 3 days Sept.	3 parents and staff	decorations food flowers film	$130	weekly Sept./May

MY GOALS BLUEPRINT

Goal	Subgoals	Action Steps	Time Needed	Resources Needed			Evaluation Checkpoints
				People	Materials	$$	

Developing goals for my professional and personal life

We are often admonished that "there is more to life than just work," or that we should "work to live, not live to work." But work and enjoyment need not be mutually exclusive. Work done to the best of our ability is one of the most satisfying of human endeavors. Our aim should be not to try to avoid work, but to find the kind of match in our professional life where our work becomes an extension of our personality, as well as helping us achieve self-respect and make a useful and necessary contribution to humanity. Real success is doing what we like and making a living at it! Our goals, then, must be in harmony with our values, needs, and resources for the proper match to result.

But those professional goals must also be in harmony with our personal goals or that professional-personal tug-of-war we described earlier will surely result. That is why a comprehensive goals blueprint for the future must weave together aspects of both our professional and personal worlds. Only in that way will our goals be in consonance.

Current research on burnout reveals that individuals most susceptible to its devastating effects are those whose entire life is consumed by their job and whose only source of recognition and gratification is their career. The best hedge against stress and overload my well be taking the time to enrich our outside interests, developing a network of supportive relationships. In other words, if we put all our eggs in one basket, measuring "success" only by what we accomplish on the job, we create a tremendous pressure on ourself. What we do in our leisure time can be just as essential to our "success" as what we do during our working time. We must develop an interest in our *self*.

Self-interest is not the same as selfishness. Maintaining a degree of detachment from our work is necessary for our emotional welfare. It is crucial that we not let our personal life be preempted by our professional life. We need and deserve time for solitude and silence, time for socializing, and time for developing the friendships that form the constellation that keeps us together. We need to develop ways both physically and mentally to "decompress"—switch gears—between the time we leave our job and when we arrive home.

Many people plan their work and education but not their leisure or social life. They may plan a vacation during the year but ignore the need for scheduling regular relaxation time during the rest of the year. These activities often get jammed into weekends between the lawn mowing, grocery shopping, and soccer game, or end up not happening at all.

Someday, we tell ourselves, we will take that Chinese cooking class, learn calligraphy, grow prize-winning petunias, learn Spanish, or stop smoking. Our imaginations overflow with possibilities but our resolve to get started is often lacking. Other time pressures and the urgency of the immediate supercede these individual needs.

The same thing occurs with respect to family goals. We echo familiar words and phrases like love, happiness, devotion, close-knit, good communication, safe and secure. But seldom do we take the time to ask ourselves what we *really* mean by these abstractions and what concrete steps we can take *today* to bring us closer to achieving them. We recognize the importance of these kinds of goals yet we also know that they rarely "just happen." Unless we can outline specific incremental steps for bringing them into reality, these goals will remain elusive and slip away unfulfilled.

Beyond our immediate family, we usually feel some commitment to outside organizations that share our values and social and political concerns. But too often we volunteer time to an array of causes we only halfheartedly support. We feel that participation in a particular organization would look good on our resume, or perhaps a friend suggested that it would be in our "best interest" to join. Or maybe we just couldn't muster up the courage to say "no" when asked if we would "help out." Whatever the reason, if we want to keep our personal-professional tug-of-war in check, we have to define precisely what our interests are and to what extent we are willing to devote a part of ourselves to each cause tugging at our sleeves.

Planning for Priorities

"Failing to plan means planning to fail."

We have moved along the path to gaining control of our time. By charting our goals for the future, we have set ourselves in the right direction. Now we must connect those future points with the present by outlining the events and activities that should happen and the conditions under which we would like them to happen. Taking the time to plan is the backbone of good time management. Most of us understand the positive and preventive benefits of planning. But too often we get so caught up in our daily routine and responsibilities and just surviving the urgent crises of today that planning gets neglected.

The irony is that the more frazzled and pressured we are, the more essential it is for us to plan our time wisely. Planning helps us keep from getting sidetracked. It helps us organize our commitments so that we can consolidate, delegate, and deal with our responsibilities before they turn into crises.

Planning need not be complex. It simply means thinking about the future in some systematic way to come up with a formula for dealing with "tomorrow" before it occurs. Only in this way can we be prepared, relaxed, and in control.

Efficiency vs. effectiveness

Good planning is not random. It proceeds along well-defined lines. At its heart lies an important management principle—the fine distinction between *efficiency* and *effectiveness*. Peter Drucker, the father of organizational management, put it this way, "It is more important to do the right thing than to do things right."[5]

Efficiency is concerned with doing things right. Effectiveness is doing the right things. While this principle has been applied widely to management theory in industry and business, it applies equally well to early childhood education. Program survival in many cases depends on teachers and directors grasping this important distinction.

Efficiency is sometimes referred to as "cost effectiveness." It concerns the cost of doing something or the way resources are utilized as measured in terms of money, materials and labor required. To be efficient is to use the fewest resources for any given task. To be effective, on the other hand, is to achieve a desired objective. While it is important to be efficient, it is even more important to be effective. Many people set out to become more efficient in the belief that in doing so they will automatically become effective. But it does not always follow.

There are numerous situations in child care where this distinction is important. The goals we set and how we decide to accomplish them can have a strong impact on the success of a program. We should first focus on effectiveness, then on efficiency—determine what we should be doing, then how to do it most efficiently. Real success is doing the *right* things *right!*

Closely related to the efficiency/effectiveness distinction is another principle derived from management theory: the 80/20 rule. It evolved from the work of Vilfredo Pareto, a 19th-century Italian economist. Pareto observed that 80 percent of his country's wealth was concentrated in the hands of 20 percent of the people. But the Pareto Principle appears to apply to countless other aspects of our lives as well: 80 percent of the teachers' time is taken up by 20 percent of the students; 80 percent of the fund-raising is done by 20 percent of the families; 80 percent of the complaints come from 20 percent of the parents.

Effective directors and teachers put Pareto's Principle to work *for* them. They realize that most of the results they achieve are produced by a few critical activities. They do not waste time on trivia, instead focusing their efforts on worthwhile strategic matters. The Pareto Principle of the "vital few" means that usually a few vital activities are critical to program success. And if we can identify these high-value activities, we will have the formula for successful time management. The answer lies in identifying our priorities and focusing on them.

Focusing on priorities

Setting priorities means making choices about how we spend our time both at work and in our personal lives. Most people set priorities in terms of urgency—the report that must get filed, the toilet that is overflowing, the laundry that is piling up. But people who set priorities according to urgency only end up dealing with the immediate and may never get started on the important.

There is a myriad of relatively unimportant matters clamoring our attention each day in the guise of being urgent. And we experience much tension each day in trying to distinguish between urgent and important matters. Our difficulty is that important matters seldom must be done today, or even this week. Urgent things, however, scream for our attention. What we need, then, is a plan for distinguishing between the urgent and important in our lives and the discipline to do the important things first. In doing so, we can break the tyranny of the urgent and begin to solve our time management problems.[6]

The key to successful utilization of time is to identify those tasks that are most vital to the success of our program (or personal life) and focus a commensurate amount of time on them. This implies a time/benefit ratio emphasizing that the time allocated to any given task should equal the potential gain. The first step is to isolate criteria for classifying and evaluating activities. Exercise 22 has been designed to help in that process. The examples in this exercise are drawn from the many roles and responsibilities in a child care setting. The same principles apply, however, to your personal world, so you might want to repeat the exercise with that in mind.

Exercise 22
My activity-rating inventory

List all the activities that you can think of that are currently waiting your attention and need to be done. Place them in one of the following four categories. Remember, important things are those events that contribute significantly to your goals. They have high value because they have long-term consequences that make a difference. Urgent things, on the other hand, have short-term consequences. They must be done now and can't wait. They may or may not be important and contribute to your goals.

Your list will include the routine (like ordering supplies, repairing a broken trike, writing a letter of reference for a past employee, or filling out the quarterly tax return) to the urgent and pressing (calling the plumber for the plugged sink, getting the payroll out, or interviewing a new teacher).

Column A we appropriately call crises; handling an irate parent, tracking down a lost reimbursement check from the state, or locating substitutes for three teachers out sick. Their resolution needs immediate attention. They are urgent as well as important.

Our difficult decisions in allocating time wisely usually come in distinguishing items between categories B, C, and D. These cover a range of possibilities from staff training, conferencing with parents, and developing curriculum materials to making the coffee, sorting the mail, and socializing with colleagues. For each teacher and director the array of possibilities will be different. Only you know what results you want and how important any particular task is in the range of tasks that determine the success of your program.

Learning to work on a priority basis requires thoughtful analysis. It also requires constant attention and comparison. When we are tempted to deviate from our plan, we need to stop and ask ourselves: "Is what I am about to do more or less important than what I had planned to do?" To be an effective tool for allocating time, setting priorities must be molded into our every day work habits. For when we fail to set priorities and work selectively our efforts are fragmented. We fall easy prey to time-consuming interruptions and end up drifting from one task to another leaving many of them unfinished. By concentrating our energies on a limited number of high-impact tasks, we can accomplish more in a shorter period of time than the person who toils many more hours each week at less important tasks.

A important and urgent	B important but not urgent	C not important but urgent	D not important and not urgent

Scheduling Time

Now that we know the fundamentals of good planning and setting priorities, it is time we convert those principles into a workable action plan. Nothing gets done by itself—we have to make it happen. If we don't take the vital step of determining precisely when the high priority activities we have isolated should be done, it will be all too easy to continue putting them off, telling ourselves "some day I'll get around to it."

Effective scheduling means transferring our "mental in-basket" to paper. This step is crucial because it helps us clarify our thoughts, commit our time, and keep from getting sidetracked. In this section we will focus our attention on a *weekly time target* and a *daily time target*. Together, these will become the axis around which our scheduling revolves.

Using these scheduling tools helps us project forward our work commitments so we can pace our activities and conserve time over-all. Pacing means completing a report before its deadline so that we might have time to send it to a typist instead of doing it ourselves at the last minute. A report mailed on time may also save a last-minute trip to the post office and the extra postage for special handling. Without this forecasting perspective in scheduling, we frequently make more work for ourselves. Take for example the person who does not schedule ahead the few minutes to renew a driver's license. This lack of scheduling may mean a missed deadline and an extra couple of hours to stand in line to take the driver's test.

This overview of our commitments also helps us see how we can group, consolidate, and rearrange our time to be more productive. For example, by simply scheduling visitors, meetings, and events that require our best appearance on only one or two days during the week, we can reduce the need to wash our hair and get spiffed up on several different days. All scheduling strategies are not quite so apparent, but if we conscientiously work to develop this perspective we will begin to see other opportunities to use our time wisely.

Many teachers and directors find that by doing their planning at the end of the day for the following day, they get a psychological head start on the next day as well. Swinging into action as soon as they arrive in the morning, they are less likely to come unglued at the dozen things waiting for their attention the moment they walk through the door. With priorities already set, they can make rational, calm decisions about what activities warrant their time and attention and how they will channel their energies during the day.

Targeting prime time

Scheduling time is far more than merely filling in the hours with meetings, calls, and appointments on our time targets. It means deliberately scheduling time to do our A- and B-priority items. It means scanning the week in advance to reserve chunks of prime time when we can work on the key activities that further our goals. If we are going to accomplish our high-value activities, we must plot time to fulfill these goals first, then schedule the remainder of our responsibilities around them.

The constant swirl of activities in a child care center makes this method of scheduling time imperative. Too many of us rationalize that our work situation is unique and too difficult to schedule in this way. But if we don't deliberately schedule our time commitments, it is all too easy to fall into a haphazard approach that results in overemphasizing daily maintenance tasks and neglecting the activities that determine the success of our program.

The difficulty comes in trying to balance contact time (for interacting with people) with concentration time (for thinking and focusing attention). Personal contact with parents, staff, and children is at the heart of the director's role in a child care center. It is essential that directors plan on time during the day when they will be available to meet parents, greet visitors, and deal with the problems of coordinating staff. But this time can eat up the entire day if we let it. We need also to schedule uninterrupted prime time to work on projects and activities that take our full undivided attention.

By analyzing your own time log you will see the pattern that is most logical for you. The key, however, is establishing a routine that works. Perhaps you could schedule your contact time around arrival and dismissal periods and block in uninterrupted concentration time in between. The pattern should become a routine that you can stick to and that others will respect because you are consistent and fair in your allocation of time.

Of course, these schedules always look precise and logical on paper. Implementing them is another matter. Unproductive, low-priority activities like opening the mail, shuffling papers, and making lengthy telephone calls creep into our schedule and do their best to lure us away from our A-priority items. We must resist the temptation to work on too many things simultaneously, not completing one task before we move on to the next. To be sure, it takes determination to stick to our schedule and not fritter away our time. But unless we make that commitment, the quality of our time will play second fiddle to its quantity. It is our decision.

Targeting time for positive self-indulgence

In his essay "In Praise of Idleness," Bertrand Russell suggests that our present economic state has put us in a paradox.[7] Our emphasis on high productivity has led to a greater number of material objects that have in turn made increasing demands on our time. "In our effort for efficiency, we are learning to make twice as many pins in a given time, not to make a given quantity of pins in half the time." Russell urges us to resist using the efficiency model to work harder and produce more, and instead to cultivate "idleness"—that positive self-indulgence that nurtures the mind and spirit. Russell may well have been espousing the best formula for burnout prevention.

But we also know that the energy and commitment required to cultivate the mind and spirit are not easily mobilized after a long, hard day at work. That is why we must take deliberate steps to carve out time for creative and recuperative growth. Our sample time log demonstrates that between work commitments, personal hygiene, eating, and house maintenance, we may have one to two hours a day at most to do the things that strengthen and satisfy us. If these few hours are not carefully scheduled, they can easily get lost in the maze of our busy schedules.

Managing our personal time means consciously setting aside a portion of each day for pursuits that enrich our minds and replenish our spirit—the kind of renewal that makes us enthusiastic about living. William Glasser calls these commitments to self "positive addictions."[8] Others have used the term "stress valves." Whatever we label them, it is crucial that they be unrelated to our work and evolve from our own interest and goals. Ceramics, guitar, yoga, meditation, photography, or jogging—the particular outlet is secondary. What is important is that we are focusing on our internal needs—that we see ourselves moving forward, reaching out, and expanding our sphere of gratification.

Exercise 23
My weekly time target

By looking at the week as a whole and seeing all our commitments for that block of time, we have a much clearer picture of how they relate to one another. It allows us to analyze the full range of responsibilities that we feel need to be done. Organizing them in a logical fashion can do much to minimize frustration.

How to use your weekly time target:

At the end of each week, write down your goals and subgoals for the following week. As you do this, think about your monthly, quarterly, and annual goals as well. This will help you keep your week in perspective. Now list all the activities needed to complete your subgoals and estimate the completion time for each task. Think in terms of absolute minimums. In other words, if you could work at this activity without any distractions, how long would it take you to complete it? Remember, your estimated time should be commensurate with the value or priority you have assigned to this task.

This time frame structures our week, making the total scope of our commitments more manageable. Our time estimates guide us in allocating our time. When we plot these estimates on our daily time target later, we'll make the adjustments to allow for interruptions and other routine matters that have to be attended to.

Weekly Time Target

For the week of _____

My goals _____
_____
_____

Activities required to accomplish my goals	Notes	Priority	Time estimate

Meetings

Telephone calls

Exercise 24
My daily time target

Having the broad picture of what needs to be accomplished for the entire week, we can now schedule our commitments for individuals days. It is essential to write this daily plan of action because few of us can possibly remember all the things we need to do. Why clutter our heads with things that can be written down? Once on paper, we can free ourselves to think of other worthwhile things (or nothing at all). Writing things down helps us clarify our thoughts and focus on the results we want. Writing increases our commitment to our schedule, and also serves as a reminder throughout the day of what we ought to be doing.

An integral part of our daily time target is the to-do list. Everyone knows about to-do lists; the big difference is how people use them. Poor time managers scrawl their daily to-do reminders on napkins, envelopes, or miscellaneous slips of paper that are often misplaced or lost. They forget appointments and responsibilities, and are inconsistent in their approach from one day to the next.

A good to-do list, on the other hand, serves as a road map to accomplishment. It is tied to a daily schedule that keeps commitments on track and structures time realistically. The useful to-do list is on a single piece of paper which is carried everywhere. The daily list can then become far more than a random collection of activities that need to be done. It also can serve as a reference to later events and a guide to future planning.

We needn't list *every* routine thing we do each day (like fluff the pillows or feed the cat), but the list must include all our A- and B-priority items. Our appointments, meetings, luncheons and other responsibilities are listed as needed.

Caution . . . Trying to schedule too much on our daily time target can be a one-way ticket to frustration! One of the biggest mistakes people make is to allocate every minute of their day. They draw up a to-do list that would most likely take three to four days to complete. They seldom accomplish what they set out to in a day and transfer too many items to the following day's time target. It is not surprising that they end up disappointed with their scheduling efforts.

When we try to cram too many things into one day, we lose sight of the fact that it is impossible to control the entire day. Good scheduling means being flexible enough to accommodate whatever situation may arise. If we fill up every moment with appointments and obligations, we're bound to feel frustrated and have our effectiveness diminished. 20 percent of our day should remain unplanned. This will leave room for the unexpected and reduce the frazzled feeling that comes from overscheduling.

Good time targets are drawn up with realistic expectations. They provide deadlines that are reasonable and achievable. They promote a psychological pat on the back when we scratch off another item on our daily time target that has moved us a small step toward achieving one of our goals.

Good time targets are also tailored to meet our individual needs. A director of a center has scheduling needs different than teachers. If we·have children of our own and many outside obligations, our needs will be different still. And it is imperative that our time target reflect our total commitments. It must weave together our professional and personal worlds into one carefully sculptured plan. Only in this way can we reduce the tug-of-war that exists between our two sides and create harmony in coordinating our many responsibilities.

Finally, keep in mind that using our time targets wisely is not the same as being inflexible. Spontaneity is a trait we also want to preserve; we want to avoid becoming a slave to our time schedules. Whatever your situation and whatever kind of daily time target you ultimately devise to meet your needs, remember that this is only a tool to help you manage your life. It should not control you.

Daily Time Target

for _____

Things to do	Priority	Time needed	Done
_____	_____	_____	☐
_____	_____	_____	☐
_____	_____	_____	☐
_____	_____	_____	☐
_____	_____	_____	☐
_____	_____	_____	☐
_____	_____	_____	☐
_____	_____	_____	☐

Meetings and conferences

_____	_____	_____	☐
_____	_____	_____	☐
_____	_____	_____	☐

Telephone calls

_____	_____	_____	☐
_____	_____	_____	☐
_____	_____	_____	☐
_____	_____	_____	☐
_____	_____	_____	☐

Follow-up

_____

_____

_____

Notes to myself

_____

_____

_____

My Schedule Today

6:00 _____

6:30 _____

7:00 _____

7:30 _____

8:00 _____

8:30 _____

9:00 _____

9:30 _____

10:00 _____

10:30 _____

11:00 _____

11:30 _____

12:00 _____

12:30 _____

1:00 _____

1:30 _____

2:00 _____

2:30 _____

3:00 _____

3:30 _____

4:00 _____

4:30 _____

5:00 _____

5:30 _____

6:00 _____

6:30 _____

7:00 _____

7:30 _____

8:00 _____

8:30 _____

9:00 _____

9:30 _____

10:00 _____

10:30 _____

11:00 _____

Notes to Myself

My Can't-Do-Without-It Plan Book

Beyond scheduling weekly and daily commitments, time management means organizing those other elements of our lives that have a direct bearing on how well we can plan our commitments. The best way to pull all these various strands together is by compiling a personalized plan book. If organized and used properly, you'll find that you *can't do-without-it* because it will be the link that connects your professional and personal life in a meaningful way.

Ideally, a plan book should be small enough to carry around with you everywhere you go. For women who carry purses this is no problem. Men will probably want to carry it in their jacket pocket. Your plan book can be adapted from one of the many planning/calendar guides on the market, perhaps in a small ringed binder or otherwise customized to your specifications.

Some things your plan book might include are:

• The bulk of a plan book should be a section holding your *weekly time target,* your *daily time target,* and a *yearly calendar* with dates filled in for school holidays, pay days, special occasions, anniversaries, birthdays, important events, and due dates for books or items on loan. These three planning guides work together to provide a systematic approach for short and long-term planning.

• Ever catch yourself having to mail a letter to a relative or friend and not having their address handy? Your plan book should include a section for *addresses* (probably no more than thirty) of the people you are most likely to send a package or letter to when away from your home or office. It should also include the addresses of everyone on your immediate staff.

• Think of how much time you spend looking up telephone numbers (or pestering the information operator) when you're away from your home or office. Your plan book should include an alphabetical telephone numbers section that might be labeled *my personal yellow pages.* It should include only essential numbers that you call regularly, possibly the following:

- 30 closest friends
- major airlines
- restaurants you frequent more than once a year
- businesses you refer to regularly for office or school supplies, general maintenance, landscape materials, etc.
- department and variety stores you shop at more than twice a year
- automobile association/towing service
- hospital and ambulance service
- police or sheriff's department
- church or religious organizations you attend
- your bank or savings & loan
- post office, florist, cleaners
- your doctor, dentist, veterinarian
- athletic club
- a list of substitute teachers and their rate of pay

• We are often called on to provide information on forms for banks, businesses, and associations that we seldom have handy when we need it. For this reason, a good plan book includes a section for *the vitals* that includes information such as the following:

- credit card numbers
- medical identification number
- insurance policy numbers
- passport number
- social security/draft card number
- savings and checking account number
- car registration and auto license number
- automobile association membership number
- membership numbers assigned for clubs, organizations
- library card number

"The vitals" could be coordinated with your telephone section. If you feel uneasy about carrying these important statistics around with you, you might prefer a separate page with abbreviations that only you can interpret.

• Your plan book should include a small pocket in which to keep a supply of:

- stamps
- return address labels
- business cards
- a small note pad
- paper clips and rubber bands

This pocket will also come in handy for keeping incidentals like a small swatch of material you need to match or a sample button that needs a mate.

• We often forget who has borrowed books, records, and other items that belong to us. How about a section titled *on loan*, with a few blank pages to keep track of our valuables?

• Memories are notoriously unreliable when we fill out our tax returns each year. But the chore next year can be simplified considerably by keeping accurate records throughout the year. A few pages in your plan book should be devoted to expenses relating to your professional activities. Your *tax information* section might include:

- mileage that you did not receive reimbursement for
- expenses related to attending professional conferences, seminars, and workshops
- meals and lodging for attending profession-related events
- food and entertainment for school-related functions that you did not receive reimbursement for
- professional books and journals purchased
- miscellaneous work-related expenses (unreimbursed curriculum materials, supplies, gifts for staff, etc.)

- There are many activities and projects that we dream up that we hope to "get to" some day. Make a section in your plan book titled *get to*, a page or two where you can list those projects and activity ideas. You might want to include various statistics or measurements here as well, just in case one day you are at an art store with a few extra minutes to find a frame for that odd-sized portrait in your attic.

- Ever get a recommendation from a friend for a book you just must read or a restaurant that you can't miss? How about a section in your plan book labeled *musts* to keep track of these sensational recommendations?

- Include a section titled *flash!* with a few pages to jot down the creative ideas that drift into your head when you least expect them. Perhaps when you add together those flashes of brilliance, you'll have the beginnings of a best-selling novel!

- Some people carry their checkbook right in their plan book. If you control the finances in your home or school, this makes good sense. If you don't you may want to carry an extra check for emergencies.

- No plan book would be complete without a section devoted to *errands*. This is the place to keep your current shopping list, your "needs" list from school, and whatever other trips and errands you need to coordinate into your schedule.

Used conscientiously, your can't-do-without-it plan book will become a valuable tool in long and short-term planning. It will eliminate forever the need to scrawl important notes on napkins and envelopes because it will always be with you. No longer will you have to call someone back because your social calendar is at home and you are at work. Moreover, you'll be amazed at how often you will refer to notes that you jotted several months before. Your plan book will become an extension of your life both at home and at work. So make a date with yourself to compile it, tailoring it to meet your own style. It is guaranteed to become an indispensable part of your time management program.

Time Tips: A Baker's Dozen

Successfully managing our time boils down to using our problem-solving abilities to think up creative ways to streamline, eliminate, and otherwise rearrange our activities to stretch our day. The formula is different for each person. What works well for one may only hinder another.

Here are a few suggestions to help you generate your own time-saving file of ideas.

1. *Group and consolidate activities:* Each time we switch to a new activity it requires a shift in our frame of mind. Grouping, consolidating, and organizing our time minimizes the need to shift our attention so often. Doing like tasks together helps make our day less fragmented and hectic. If you have a number of phone calls to make, gather together the numbers and do them all at once. If you have several letters to write, sit down and do them together. The same thing holds true for filing or cataloging books and materials. Your weekly action plan will help you spot areas where you can consolidate errands, appointments, and miscellaneous activities, saving transportation time and inefficiency.

Group activities also saves in "prep time" because we will be gathering the materials we need (like the stamps, stationery, and envelopes for writing letters) only once. Many teachers find that when they save all their professional journals for one scheduled work session a month they can get through them faster than if they read them randomly. By organizing all the things they need in one sitting, they can clip and save and up-date their curriculum ideas file all at once.

2. *Get a good start.* Frantic mornings at home can set the stage for a chaotic day. But getting a relaxed start in the morning can be nothing short of a miracle, particularly when there are children to get ready. We all know mornings are the time when the button pops or the zipper breaks. While no one has come up with the perfect solution for dawdling kids or that fickle finger of fate that immobilizes the car battery, a bit of preplanning can take much of the hassle out of morning routines and help us deal with the unexpected more calmly.

Planning the night before pays off. The coffee pot can be plugged in, lunches made, clothes set out, and accessories planned. These activities which take so little time in the evening can give us a running start on the morning.

The same principle applies to the classroom, where perhaps the most important fifteen minutes of the day is the quarter hour before the children arrive. Preplanning means that we are in control, prepared to handle any mini-disaster. If we are still preoccupied with making coffee, mixing paint, or running off a ditto when the children arrive, we won't be available to greet them and set the tone for a calm, relaxed day. Arrival time is when we might anticipate difficulty in separating from parents, or when parents may want to talk to us. If we are still scurrying about, we have not only shortchanged the parents and their children but ourselves because we have started the day off on "the wrong foot." Our entire day is likely to stay rushed and frantic.

3. *Develop routines:* Planning so that we can do the same things at the same time each day or each week both conserves energy and promotes continuity in our lives. Regularity in routines cuts down on indecision and on hassles. This is particularly true with household chores like washing clothes and grocery shopping, but it carries over to our professional sphere as well. For instance, when we schedule field trips regularly rather than randomly, the children and other staff can prepare for them. Even if the routine is something like "every other Friday" or the "first Tuesday of the month," the parents of students can coordinate their schedules in advance to assist in transportation, and the other staff in our center can coordinate their activities to eliminate potential scheduling conflicts.

Developing a regular routine is the heart of establishing new habits, particularly in the area of our physical health. Scheduling that racquetball match or committing ourselves to attending an exercise class at the same time each week reduces the possibility that we'll put these activities off and never get around to them.

4. *Avoid congestion:* Crowds, long lines, and limited parking are all part of the inconvenience of modern living. While we can't eliminate them, we can take positive steps to reduce their impact. If you hate the lines at the post office, bank or supermarket, schedule these errands to avoid peak congestion periods. Buy stamps in bulk, keep a postal scale and current postal rates, and decrease the need to stand in line at the post office. Do your banking at a place that offers walk-up or drive-by tellers or instant automatic banking services. Select a grocery store where you can shop early in the morning or late in the evening. Take steps at home, also, to organize your menus in advance and coordinate buying to cut down on unnecessary trips.

Eliminate some of these errands altogether by ordering from catalogs. Stock up on cards and gifts for birthdays, anniversaries, and special occasions. Make a secret shelf in one of your closets where you can keep a supply of small favors and gifts for those last-minute thank-yous. Having items on hand will make it much easier to make these thoughtful gestures promptly.

5. *Take advantage of your mood:* From our biological rhythms self-assessment inventory, we have a good understanding of our own internal prime time. We can put this knowledge to work by scheduling activities that need our full concentration for times when we will be at our peak. In others words, to the extent possible we should match our daily time target with our energy profile. We also need to be alert to fatigue. It does little good to force ourselves to do an activity if our mind, spirit, and energy level are at their depth. Often just taking a quick break, a "mental run around the block" will help refresh us and refocus our creative energies.

6. *Coordinate personal care needs far in advance:* A little forethought in the area of health and personal-care needs can really pay off. If we plan six months in advance for hair, doctor, dentist, and any other non-emergency appointment we can schedule them at times most convenient for us. Scheduling in advance also allows us to choose our time away from the center so that it doesn't conflict with especially busy periods. Moreover, if we have the flexibility, we can request the first appointment in the morning and eliminate long waits in the waiting room.

7. *Be a wait-watcher:* Most people spend forty minutes or more each day in transition time between activities. We can't eliminate this altogether, but we can learn to use this time productively. Waiting for appointments, waiting in traffic jams, waiting for the carpool provides snatches of time to read, plan, and organize. Carry along several mini-tasks that can be done in five minutes. Or carry a book that you can read in these in-between times. Who knows, you may finish *War and Peace* while you wait at the metro station for your spouse each evening.

8. *Think about being early:* Are you a nick-of-time expert rushing from one appointment to another and always arriving just in the nick of time? Most people who are consistently late consistently underestimate the time it will take to get from Point A to Point B. The only way to break this behavior pattern is to plan backwards from departure time. Leave a large margin to account for unexpected heavy traffic, an empty gas tank, or tight parking at the destination. In other words, plan to be early. How much better to shed that nick-of-time status and trade it in for an "I can always count on you" reputation.

9. *Double your pleasure:* We don't want to be compulsive about using every single minute of the day, but when we can schedule time to accomplish more in less, let's do it. Commute time provides us with the perfect opportunity to learn Spanish, listen to lectures, or record our thoughts if we have a cassette play/recorder in our car. If you entertain frequently, plan a dinner menu that you can double so you can entertain on consecutive evenings.

10. *Call ahead:* We waste a lot of time when people forget or are late for appointments. A quick phone call to remind visitors of a scheduled tour of your facility, to parents to double-check on a prearranged conference, and to other people to confirm appointments is not only a courtesy but a help in budgeting our time.

The same principle applies to other areas of planning. We can call ahead to have a supplies order waiting when we stop by the stationery store. We can call the deli to prepare that hero sandwich ahead of time, or the pharmacy to refill our prescription. Better yet, why not take advantage of delivery services when they're available? The small charge for the convenience may far outweigh the cost in time to do the errand ourselves.

11. *Those bits and pieces add up:* Time to do anecdotal progress notes on students is difficult to fit into our schedules. One clever solution adopted by an enterprising teacher is to carry around several small sheets of address labels (The 1½" × 3" size). At miscellaneous free moments, use these to jot down a note about a child's progress. Once a month peel them off and put them in the appropriate child's file. It is amazing how those bits and pieces add up to a full anecdotal record by the end of the school year.

12. *Become a speed reader:* Coping with information overload is inherent in our profession. Keeping on top of current advocacy issues, research on child development, and new trends in curriculum methods of instruction is time-consuming as well. It also leaves little time for other literary interest outside of our profession. Applying the tips and techniques taught in speed-reading courses can be immensely helpful in getting a handle on the volume of material we want to read. Consciously push yourself to speed up your rate of reading. Avoid rereading paragraphs. Try not to subvocalize. Read for key ideas and the main point of an article instead of reading it in its entirety. Skim the table of contents, glance at chapter headings, and read only those parts necessary for you to gain the information you need. But most important, work at building your concentration skills while you read. Much time is lost in reading because our attention wanders and we lose comprehension. If we work to recall and retain, our reading time becomes purposeful time and time well spent.

13. *Eliminate when possible:* An often neglected area of time management is structuring ways to eliminate or at least radically reduce the amount we do. For example, is that beautiful lawn that requires weekly mowing absolutely necessary, or is low-maintenance ground cover just as attractive? The same principle applies to our classroom environment or center operation. Here we have to make sure that our trade-offs don't sacrifice quality for economy. But it may be possible, for instance, that nine news-letters are just as effective in communicating school events as twelve; that ten field trips are just as rewarding as fifteen; or that three cooking projects per week will reach our nutrition objectives just as well as five. Take a close look. Search out clues as to how you can eliminate unnecessary procedures, committees, activities, and events, yet still maintain your standards.

Clearing the Hurdles

Carefully outlining our goals, planning priorities, and targeting our time does not necessarily mean that our path to gaining control of our time will be free of obstacles. Untimely interruptions, inability to say "no", the incessant telephone, and our tendency to procrastinate are a few of the stumbling blocks that crop up. But if we are prepared with concrete strategies for dealing with them, it is possible to overcome these obstacles and keep on track to a balanced life.

Avoiding interruptions

Frequent, time-consuming interruptions may well be one of the accepted "givens" inherent in the nature of the child care director's role. But that is not to say that interruptions cannot be controlled and reduced to a manageable few. Our self-assessment time log has provided us with insights as to the type and frequency of interruptions we encounter during a typical day. And we have seen how targeting our time more wisely and not trying to do high concentration tasks when there are bound to be interruptions can go a long way to reducing frustration on the job.

The key to managing interruptions is to develop a system of "planned unavailability" times matched with other times where the director is accessible, and ready to handle any interruptions. Nonverbal signals like a closed door or a small but conspicuous sign that says *"Do not disturb"* can convey the seriousness of these "unavailable" times.

But these periods of unavailability must be balanced with sufficient time where the administrator is truly available. If a director establishes available times that can be counted on, staff and parents can usually structure their time to coincide.

Many times when people interrupt they are not necessarily being inconsiderate. They may just be unaware of our many responsibilities. Certainly more than a dash of diplomacy is necessary to convey the pressures and deadlines we face. These situations require tact and thoughtful communication skills. Speaking up for our own rights without stepping on the rights of others can improve over-all staff relations while helping us control our time and increase effectiveness.

Learning to say "no" with sensitive assertiveness

Perhaps the most effective time-saving tip of all is the frequent and judicious use of the word "no." We cannot protect our priorities unless we learn to tactfully refuse requests that do not further our goals. But we often feel guilty when we say "no." We fear hurting people's feelings, alienating them, and making enemies.

Developing the ability to say "no" is one of the most difficult skills to acquire. It takes time, experience, and no small amount of self-assurance. But people who lack the conviction to assert themselves wind up living their lives according to other people's priorities.

"No" is not a nasty word. It does not mean that we are insensitive and uncaring. In fact, the most thoughtful thing we can do is to be honest and responsible to both ourself and others. We can learn to say "no" without offending. Here are a few suggestions: Listen carefully to the request to show the other person you understand what is being asked. Then say "No" immediately. Don't build up false hopes. Give reasons only if you feel it is necessary, but be careful they don't sound like lame excuses. When possible, offer alternatives to show you care.

Taming the telephone

The telephone has been dubbed "the greatest nuisance among conveniences and the greatest convenience among nuisances."[9] When our friend Alexander Graham Bell invented the telephone, he thought he was giving the world a useful tool. But many people regard this marvelous instrument as a kind of tyrant that invades privacy, forever interrupting our work and concentration.

One way to master the telephone is to analyze incoming calls. Just how much of our time is eaten up by calls that could be handled by someone else? How many calls are we getting for information about our center that could be mailed out? We may find that it saves time to invite inquiring callers to the school for a firsthand tour. Scheduling a half dozen visitors on one occasion saves us from repeating the essentials of our program over and over.

A call-back system is also extremely helpful. When we stop to analyze our calls, we will probably see that there are very few that have to be handled immediately. If our calls are screened and callers told precisely what time we'll be returning phone calls, we can block out a period of time to handle them. Answering services and answering machines can serve the same function.

Many directors who have more than one facility have found that conference calls (placed through the operator) are an extremely efficient way of conducting business. They not only eliminate duplication but allow matters to be concluded far more quickly and with clearer understanding between everyone concerned.

Try placing your telephone calls between 8:00 and 9:00 a.m. Since most people are eager to get going in the morning, they are more apt to make these early morning calls short and to the point. Begin your conversation with, "Is this a good time to talk?" This expression of courtesy will be returned by people that you deal with regularly on the telephone. It will give you the opportunity to tactfully reply, "No, I'm sorry, I'm in the middle of a project at the moment. May I return your call at 11:00?" If we let people rattle on when it is not convenient, we are not really doing them or ourselves a favor.

It is also helpful to let the other person know at the *beginning* of the conversation what your time constraints are. If you have only a few minutes to talk before you have to leave the office, attend a meeting, or get back to the children, say so promptly.

Finally, we need to let our colleagues know that we respect them more than we do the telephone. How often do we interrupt a conference or meeting to answer a telephone call? We wouldn't let another person barge into the room and interrupt our conversation, but somehow we accord instant attention to our telephone. Sometimes it is true that there is no one to cover the telephone while we meet with a colleague or parent. But even in these cases, it is only common courtesy to terminate the call as quickly as possible or let the caller know when we can call back.

Springing the procrastination trap

"What one postpones, one abandons."
                                        Peter Drucker

Procrastination plagues all of us and is one of the major stumbling blocks in learning to manage time effectively. We are told that the National Association of Procrastinators boasts a membership of well over 15,000. "However," clarifies the President, "only a small handful of our followers have gotten around to paying their dues." Increasingly popular these days, also, are the round buttons displaying the bold letters TUIT—especially designed for people who never manage to get "around to it."

Procrastination is sharpening our pencils when we should be tackling a report. It is watching "just one more" program on television when we should be doing the dishes. Procrastination comes in an array of clever disguises, but the guilt and worry that result are universal. Many people quickly deal with occasional lapses into procrastination and momentum is restored. But for others, procrastination is not occasional. It is a well-established behavior pattern where the concern over uncompleted tasks turns to increased self-recrimination for not having the resolve to break out of the cycle. For these individuals, procrastination doesn't just nibble away their time, it gobbles it away and prevents them from achieving their goals.

I AM GOING TO STOP PUTTING THINGS OFF

STARTING TOMORROW

maybe

Exercise 25
My procrastination profile

Analyze your own procrastination habits by asking yourself the following questions:

1. What kinds of activities do I tend to put off most frequently?

2. What excuses or rationalizations do I engage in to justify my postponing activities that I know I should be doing?

3. How do I feel about my delay tactics—would I like to change them and stop procrastinating?

4. How is my procrastinating affecting others?

5. Do I tend to procrastinate more at the beginning of a project or get bogged down part way through a task?

6. What do I do when I am procrastinating— do I suddenly feel fatigued and find an excuse to nap? Do I get great hunger pangs and reach for a candy bar? Or do I engage in "filler" activities like straightening my desk or doing low priority paper work?

7. What task am I currently avoiding?

Once we have isolated our own procrastinating tendencies, it is easier to pinpoint the causes and develop workable solutions for preventing the behavior. In fact, for many people, just recognizing their early warning signals (those "filler" or "escape" behaviors) helps them circumvent the onset of procrastination. Now let's tackle the four major reasons why people put things off and offer guidelines to overcoming and changing these patterns.

Avoiding the unpleasant: There are many things we must do in our lives that are just plain unpleasant. Procrastinating distasteful tasks ranks high on everyone's list of time wasters. The irony is that we feel that by postponing an unpleasant task we are making life easier. But putting off the distasteful only increases the problem because tasks that fall in this category seldom disappear. For example, rather than confronting the unsatisfactory performance of a child care aide, a director will avoid facing the issue in the hope that things will improve. They rarely do. Instead, resentment and anger build and the situation can become far more explosive the longer we delay.

The balance-sheet method of analyzing the pros and cons works remarkably well when we are confronted with an unpleasant task. When tallied, the positive and negative effects that accrue by doing the "thing" now or postponing it usually reveal a strikingly obvious answer. Delay usually only worsens the situation and increases our tension.

Sometimes just thinking of the euphoria that comes from promptly tackling the unpleasant matter is enough incentive to move us into action. At other times, we may have to promise ourselves some kind of "jelly bean" as a reward for handling the situation.

If sometimes we do the unpleasant task first, the worry and guilt is lifted from our shoulders and we sail through the day burden-free. Stressing the benefits of not delaying the unpleasant can strengthen our fortitude in the future, because we are able then to build on that experience.

Being overwhelmed by the enormity of the task: Many of us consistently underestimate the amount of time different projects and activities take. So we build up a negative system of responses and delay getting started on something new. We develop a wonderful repertoire of excuses to justify our procrastination: "I haven't got all the materials I need to get started," "I have to wait until I can block out a whole period of uninterrupted time to tackle this one," etc., etc. It is true that most people will not start a project they believe they can't finish, so they tend to postpone getting started until their delay turns into a crisis and they are forced to act.

Many times just setting a realistic deadline for the task helps us get started. Even self-imposed deadlines can shake us out of our state of inertia. Going public by letting other people know about our deadlines also helps because it creates added support (and subtle pressure). But more often than not, we avoid difficult tasks because we simply do not know where to begin.

When confronted with what seems like an overwhelming project, many procrastinators find strength in the following homily shared by marathon runners. When asked by a reporter how they managed to complete the grueling 26-mile course, one lanky marathoner responded, "How do you eat an elephant? One bite at a time!" This may well be the best method for attacking that dreaded task.

Begin by asking yourself just what is the final result you want to achieve. Then work backwards, breaking the task down into as many definable parts as possible. Put these in sequential order of how they need to be done. Some people call this the "swiss cheese" approach. By poking holes into the whole, you may discover that the project is far less difficult than you expected.

If this divide-and-conquer method still doesn't provide the necessary motivation, try doing a preliminary task like sorting the necessary materials or taking notes on points to be covered. Promise yourself you'll do it for just five minutes. What you may find is that the project isn't quite as foreboding as it appeared, and once you get moving you may be tempted to try for another five minutes.

Striving for perfection: Closely tied to avoiding the overwhelming task is another cause of procrastination, striving for perfection. Many of us have a compelling desire to do a job perfectly or not at all. But striving for perfection is not the same as striving for excellence.[10] Perfectionism comes from setting impossibly high standards for ourselves. Instead of motivating us, it tends to paralyze us.

We say to ourselves that we should write that thank you note to our aunt for the birthday gift. But a short note won't suffice for such a nice gift. So we put off writing until we have more time to write a perfect thank you. That time never comes, of course, so we find ourselves saddled with a new problem. Not only haven't we written, but an embarrassing amount of time has lapsed. So, we rationalize, instead of writing a one-page letter we will make up for the delay by writing a newsy three-page letter. Our procrastination has increased our burden. In all likelihood, we'll delay even further because we've now created an overwhelming task for ourselves—one that will take even more time. When we finally break down from the weight of our guilt, we apologize profusely and resolve to never let this predicament happen again. If we analyze our procrastination pattern in this case, we realize that, like many of our justifications, it was based on a faulty premise—that perfection was more important than promptness.

In a country that fosters perfectionism in many subtle ways, it takes a lot of courage to be less than perfect. If we are going to conquer procrastination, however, we must tackle head on our devotion to over-organization, over-cleanliness, and over-conscientiousness. We have to expose them for what they are—unrealistic roadblocks to performance. We should strive for "functional efficiency" instead and accept that we do not have to be a model of perfection to do a job that we can take pride in.

Difficulty making decisions: The final reason why many people procrastinate is that they find it difficult to make decisions. Indecisiveness can usually be traced to vague worries: fear of disapproval, failure, making a mistake, pain, rocking the boat, or confronting the unknown. Also many of us tenaciously hold on to the myth that delay improves the quality of our decisions. We end up using valuable time weighing the pros and cons of taking a wrong step. As an excuse to avoid making a decision, we profess that we need more facts. But this "paralysis of analysis" just weighs us down even more. Carried to extremes, our indecisiveness would even tell us "not to go into the water until we know how to swim."

Some argue that women in particular have a hard time making difficult decisions because they tend to take few risks, seeing them as chances to lose rather than gain something.[11] They view risk as potential loss, danger, or injury to be avoided at all cost. This error-avoidance can have ramifications in both our professional and personal lives.

At work, the tempo of a school—the speed with which an organization identifies and solves problems, makes decisions, and grasps opportunities—is a direct reflection of the attitude and style of the person in charge.[12] If the pace of that person is sluggish, indecisiveness can seep its way down through the ranks, generating a pervasive attitude of risk avoidance.

On a personal level, the same thing holds true. People that dawdle, drift, and avoid making decisions usually let life pass by while they're weighing all the alternatives. It's like the old proverb that warns, "He who waits before taking the next step spends his entire life on one leg."

But we can't deny our emotions either. What we need to do is determine which fears are real and which are exaggerated, then take steps to deal with them appropriately. Sometimes just playing out the "worst case" scenario exposes our fears for what they are and allows us to quickly dispose of exaggerated anxieties. At other times developing a "worry list" might be necessary.[13] Writing down all the things that worry us, all the horrible things that might go wrong, helps us when we reread this list periodically and note what actually happened in each case. What we'll find is that most of the things we worry about never happen. This in itself becomes a good reason for worrying less.

People who are successful make decisions quickly. Often they are wrong but they don't belabor it. They have cultivated a willingness to make mistakes. They understand that it is possible to fail and not be a failure. They take methodical steps to solve their problems and make decisions. It might be said, in fact, that they embrace the philosophy, "If you've got a problem that can't be solved, you haven't got a problem."

When we have difficulty solving a problem or making a decision, the following formula is helpful:

1. State the problem. Put it in writing as clearly and concisely as possible.

2. What are all the contributing causes of this problem? What are the main obstacles that are present? Define and isolate the who, what, when, where and why of the difficulty.

3. What are *all* the possible solutions? Play out the whole range of possibilities.

4. Evaluate the alternatives and look at the consequences of taking each action. Weigh all the advantages and disadvantages of each alternative.

5. Select the best solution. This may well be a combination of two alternatives.

6. Carry through and do it! Don't look back and don't keep weighing more alternatives. And remember the words of Henri-Frederic Amiel: "The person who insists upon seeing with perfect clearness before deciding, never decides."

In the final assessment, the best way to overcome procrastination is to work out strategies to avoid it in the first place. Recognize that nothing is so fatiguing as the hanging on of an uncompleted task and that worry is a pure and simple waste of time. If we set objectives that are right for us, priorities that are clear, and deadlines that are achievable and allow us to pace our work, we may be able to conquer procrastination once and for all.

Looking Back and Assessing Progress

Most of us need some sense of closure in our lives—time to look back over the day's events and assess just how well things went. Effective directors and teachers do this daily. They recognize that evaluation and reevaluation is a continuous process. At the end of the day they tie up loose ends, assess their accomplishments, and plan for the following day's activities. This is a routine yet vital aspect of the way they manage their lives.

Effective time managers focus on the things they *did* accomplish rather than dwell on the things they did not get to. They take a look at what they did that day that moved them closer to realizing their goals. They search out clues that help them plan their time better in the future. They engage in deliberate after-action analysis to assess the reasons why something went well, and they jot down ideas that will form the basis of planning the next time around. The checklist at the end of this section will serve as a useful guide in assessing progress.

Forecasting the future

Nothing is as simple as it seems.
   Everything takes longer than it should.
      If anything can go wrong, it will!

Murphy's Law

Few of us find comfort in chaos, yet many of us ignore the wisdom of Murphy's Law. In our personal lives the sink gets clogged, the kids lose their lunch money, a zipper breaks just as we're rushing out the door. We will never be able to keep these mini-crises from happening, but we can do a lot to reduce their impact on our lives. Most minor emergencies can be handled in such a way to curtail the stress that comes hand-in-hand with most of these panic situations.

Used properly, our weekly time target and daily time target work together as our guide for forecasting the future. From the written notes we have jotted down as part of our after-action analysis will emerge patterns that form the basis of our future planning. By pinpointing the conditions that breed our crises, we can take preventive steps to deal effectively with them. Even our random hectic days usually follow a pattern. If we can discover it, we have a powerful tool for predicting events. Only by looking back and assessing what has happened can we begin to anticipate the unanticipated, and defy Murphy's Law.

Looking for patterns in our notes also lets us appreciate that there are inevitably going to be periods when things will be busy, if not hectic. But if we can use that knowledge to our benefit, planning our time and structuring our commitments around these busy periods, we can deal with them far more easily. Oftentimes, just acknowleging that we are approaching a stressful couple of weeks helps us prepare for it psychologically and accept the inevitable more calmly. We may well find, for instance, that these occur regularly and coincide with the holidays, enrollment fluctuations, or seasonal changes in the weather.

As we look through our notes, for example, we may notice that October is an especially heavy month for illness among our staff. We can prepare for this cycle by updating our substitute list and finding additional volunteers to cover the anticipated increase in absences. Likewise, if we see that March is usually a busy month for visitors we can make sure that we schedule other events to allow us time to devote to these public relations activities.

In the final assessment, as we check our progress in managing our time, we become acutely aware that we have to budget our time as if we were paying for it. What we must look at are the psychic costs and physical wear-and-tear when we do not take time management seriously. This leads us to the inescapable conclusion that in the end time is all we have. We can't afford to be haphazard in allocating it, or it will just continue to get absorbed into the frenetic pace of our daily routine. If we don't use it wisely today, it may be gone forever.

Yesterday is a cancelled check
Tomorrow is a promissory note
Today is ready cash. Use it![14]

Exercise 26
My time management checklist

• What activities gave me the greatest source of satisfaction today?

• At what times did I feel tense and rushed today?

• How often was I late for appointments or scheduled meetings? Could this have been avoided?

• How many of my interruptions today were caused by external factors beyond my control? How many were self-generated?

• How did my actions throughout the day affect the people around me? Did I interrupt others? Sidetrack their concentration? Keep them waiting?

• Did I find myself saying "If only I had . . . ," instead of "Next time, I'll . . .?

• Did I underestimate the amount of time a task or activity would take?

• Did I finish one task before moving on to the next, or did I try to do too many things at once?

• Did I overschedule my day and try to accomplish too much?

- Did I procrastinate today? Why? What did I do?

- Did I schedule my high energy time for creative activities?

- How did I reward myself for the good things I accomplished today?

- What can I do tomorrow that will improve my effectiveness on the job?

Chapter 4
Managing Space

The Nature of Space—An Overview

Literally everything we do is associated with the experience of space. It affects what we say, how we feel, and how we behave. Sometimes the effect is positive: Think of the serene, carefree feeling that relaxes every muscle as you sit under a star-studded sky and listen to the mellow sounds at an outdoor concert. But at other

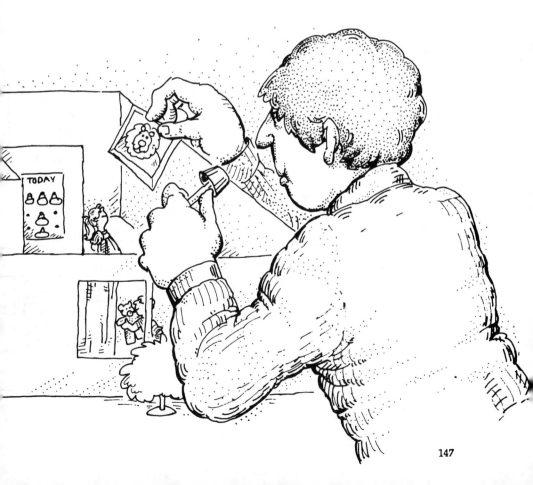

times the effect is negative: Take the claustrophobic feeling that chokes you when you sit for hours in a poorly ventilated theatre with cramped seats and narrow aisles. Our sense of space, then, is a synthesis of many sensory stimuli from our immediate environment, including visual, auditory, kinesthetic, olfactory, and thermal elements.

In some cases, environmental conditions and physical decor do not simply affect us—they control us on a subliminal level. Studies show, for example, that in grocery stores equipped with easy listening music and strategically placed items, people not only browse longer but spend more money. Moreover, the arrangement of furniture within settings can foster or discourage social relationships. A library, for instance, is arranged to discourage interaction and minimizing contact between people. Think as well of the typical arrangement for a room set up for a lecture. The spatial arrangement of chairs in straight, rigid rows not only focuses our attention on the speaker but also restricts our social interaction.

The arrangement of space can convey subtle but powerful nonverbal messages—a silent communication that often contains more information than our verbal messages. Consider the highrise structures that house many corporate offices.[1] Most often the executive suites are placed on the top floors for the ostensible advantages of privacy and view. But once this is done, the arrangement of the whole building falls into a heirarchical pattern with the status of individuals measured by their distance from the top.

John De Lorean speaks of the mystique surrounding "The Fourteenth Floor", that pinnacle of status of the corporate policy makers of General Motors.[2] Their position in the building captured the essence of power, money, and prestige that accompanied their vertical ascension on the corporate ladder. De Lorean tells how the electronically locked and guarded door, the private elevator, and the aura of secrecy enshrouding those at the top had a powerful impact on the "lower level" employees of GM as rumors about "life at the top" circulated around the corporation.

While the corporate analogy is dramatic, it is clear that the physical structure of a building affects the social system housed within it, and that physical barriers often result in a corresponding social barrier.

How people relate in space is the focus of an emerging field of inquiry, environmental psychology.[3] It recognizes that our sense of space is closely tied to our sense of self—that our "place identity" is intricately linked to the complex human activity that goes on in different settings. Environment psychologists look at concepts like personal space, territoriality, crowding, and the effects of environmental factors like heat and light seeking to integrate and connect them to various motivational factors.[4]

Research has found that our physical environment can have a strong psychological effect on our mood and work habits. Think of the frustration of trying to work in someone else's kitchen, or the physical fatigue that overcomes us when we try to concentrate in a place where the lights are glaring and the chairs uncomfortable.

It is no surprise, then, that there is a close relationship between our work environment and job productivity. Work spaces that are too crowded, too noisy, too cold or hot, too dim, or where the furniture is too difficult to maneuver around do little to contribute to worker satisfaction. In fact, such environmental stressors can be a major source of tension.

The implications for early childhood educators are clear. School design plays an important role in how happy and how productive we are on the job. Arrangements that are stressful, harmful, or otherwise unpleasant can result in costly management problems as well as excessive absenteeism, employee turnover, and job burnout.

The Microgeography of the Early Childhood Environment

An awareness of the principles of environmental psychology is particularly important because of the unique opportunity that many teachers and directors of early childhood programs have to be directly involved in the spatial considerations of a center. Unlike their colleagues who teach at the elementary or secondary level who must cope with the environmental givens of a public school building, early childhood educators are often involved in the architectural decision-making process of designing new facilities or planning major renovations on existing structures.

The term microgeography is useful to describe our task of analyzing the spatial surroundings in our centers. It includes looking at the layout of physical space, the location and interaction of people, and the flow of activities within the facility. Coupled with our experience of working with young children and a healthy dose of common sense, we can come up with the ingredients for good use of space—space that meets the needs of both adults and children.

The underlying premise of this analysis holds that the space in our centers is not neutral. It can have a positive or negative influence on our behavior. When we consider that our work environment is our home away from home, it becomes even more important to focus on the psychological effects that the organization of space has on our mood, disposition, work habits and productivity. The rationale is clearly pragmatic. How do we create quality settings where adults and children can thrive?

The quality of spatial organization has been found to relate to a variety of variables in the early childhood center. The higher the quality of space, the more child care workers are sensitive and friendly in the way they relate to one another and to the children. In positive environments, teachers are more likely to help and encourage children and to teach mutual respect and cooperation.[5]

Conversely, when the quality of spatial arrangements is low, noise level is likely to increase and children are more likely to engage in disruptive behavior. Teachers are more apt to be tired and irritable and resort to arbitrary procedures in managing children.[6]

It is not difficult to see the link between the type and quality of spatial environments in schools and stress in child care workers. Where the organization of space and materials is at odds with the needs of teachers and directors, frustration accumulates, dissatisfaction intensifies, and poor performance results.

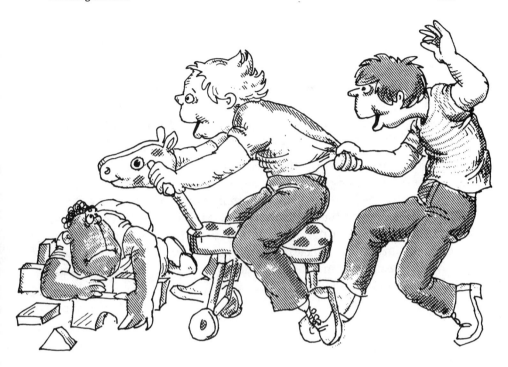

When we think about the space in an early childhood setting, we often think of adult and child space as being mutually exclusive. We have given scant attention to the spatial needs of children and even less to the needs of adults. However, the needs of adults and children often overlap and the spatial dynamics of a school are far too complex to draw clear distinctions. If we are going to have an environment for children to learn in and adults to work in, we must be concerned about meeting the needs of both.

Resolving spatial problems in the early childhood setting is not easy, though. The open and informal atmosphere that characterizes most child care environments creates problems for workers wanting to make change. It is difficult in a "shared" space to maintain control over the quality of the setting. Often decisions concerning the use of space require group action. Moreover, many teachers and directors must cope with a set of constraints like existing fixtures, odd-shaped rooms, immovable walls, and poor natural light. In addition, there may be limited funds for making improvements. But to the extent that there are changes that can be made, we ought to do what we can to maximize the use of space to achieve our goals.

What we need is to develop a shift in spatial perspective. We need first to increase our awareness of the influence of space around us, assess our spatial limitations, and finally address the needs of the users within our setting, both adults and children.

The remainder of this section on space management is devoted to building an awareness of our own setting. The space profile provided will be helpful in that task. From there, we move to a discussion of the critical dimensions that must be considered in our organization of space. Finally we will zero in on the two primary areas of concern within an early childhood center: organizing classroom space and organizing support space for administrative functions.

Exercise 27
My space profile

The following questions are designed to help you identify the areas that you feel might need attention in your work environment. Don't worry about particulars at this point. Just fill out the assessment quickly; we'll discuss specific remedies later.

My environment:	Fre-quently	Occa-sionally	Never
• The decibel level in my center could match any airport. I've contemplated earplugs.	___	___	___
• The lighting in my office/classroom makes me squint and want to wear sunglasses.	___	___	___
• The temperature in my room is so predictably cold, I keep ski gloves handy to ward off frostbite on particularly chilly days.	___	___	___
• My room is so hot and stuffy that I feel sweaty, languid, and fatigued much of the day.	___	___	___
• My center would get the "bland award" for color and variation.	___	___	___
• I feel like Gulliver in the Land of Lilliput. There is so much emphasis on child-sized furnishings that I feel awkward and out of place.	___	___	___

Exercise 28
How well do I manage my space?

	Fre-quently	Occa-sionally	Never
• My classroom is like an obstacle course. I get black & blue from tripping over children and bumping into furniture.	____	____	____
• I file things away in drawers and file cabinets but forget just where I put them when I go to find them.	____	____	____
• When I attempt to retrieve one box from my supply closet, ten more come cascading down on my head.	____	____	____
• I misplace my car keys, purse, notebook, and briefcase.	____	____	____
• I have been heard to lament that all my storage problems would disappear if I just had "one more closet."	____	____	____
• I've contemplated joining Clutterbugs Anonymous.	____	____	____

My Ideal:

There are certain things that make my favorite spot for reading and concentrating just right for me. (Describe in terms of lighting, color, texture, sunlight, plants, background music, work position, proximity to the refrigerator, etc., etc.)

Assessing the spatial organization of my work environment

Let's take a mental trip to our work environment and think about the nonverbal messages conveyed by the arrangement of our space. We know that the way we arrange, decorate, and use the space around us says a lot about our values, the way we relate to other people, and our priorities in life. The way we utilize our environment is our personal trademark of how we perceive space. So let's take a look to uncover what our work environment says about us.

First walk into the reception area of your facility. What subtle nonverbal cues would a new parent walking into this space get? Is it friendly and welcoming, chaotic, disorganized, cold, or sterile? Even seemingly insignificant things like the placement of the receptionist's desk, the arrangement of pictures on the walls and the colors of the room will all have an influence on what that first impression will be.

What nonverbal messages does this environment convey about how parents are viewed at the center? Is there an information bulletin board, parenting books, handouts, or a place for parents to meet and socialize with one another? These first impressions of the environment may be important to the success of a program. Consciously or subconsciously, many parents translate their first impressions into indicators of how well they feel their child will be cared for. If the center is disorganized and everyone is barely keeping chaos from erupting, parents may assume this haphazard manner will be the style with which children are cared for. Such first impressions can make the difference whether or not the child even gets enrolled in the school.

Now take a peek into the teacher's prep room. In some centers this is a separate room. In others, it is a lounge shared with the parents or the director. What does this space say about how teachers are valued at this center? Is there a place for a child care worker to retreat from the activity in the classroom to be alone with a warm coffee pot and professional magazines and journals? Is there an adult restroom nearby equipped with personal care items? Is there a place to make a confidential telephone call or carry on a private parent conference? Is there a place for staff to store their personal belongings?

What does this space say about the teachers' values? How do they as a group take care of the center's equipment, materials, and supplies? Are they thrifty and careful or lavish and careless in the way they use the educational materials available to them?

Now, swing into the director's office. What do the colors, displays, pictures, plants, and accessories, and arrangement of furniture reveal about this person's nature and values? Does the position of the desk and the arrangement of furniture encourage conversation? Is the office cool and shaded, sunfilled, or dark and drab? And what does the arrangement of materials say about the administrator's management and leadership skills?

Finally, move into the classroom. Kneel down to get the child's perspective of the environment. What is the child's first impression of the environment? Overwhelming, frightening, or warm and inviting? Is there friendly order or a cluttered jungle that the child must maneuver through? What displays are at the child's eye level, and what nonverbal messages does the overall spatial arrangement convey to the child?

Looking at the way the teachers and children operate within the classroom setting can also provide clues as to any spatial problems that need addressing.

• Are materials organized in a clear and consistent way to encourage self-help, or are the children dependent on the teacher for guidance? How often do you hear a child say, "Where is . . ."?

• Do children wander aimlessly or have difficulty getting started in activities? Is there a sufficient number of play units to keep all the children occupied, and does the challenge of those activities encourage sustained involvement for a period of time?

• Does the spatial arrangement of activity centers encourage or discourage social interaction between children? How often do disputes erupt over sharing of materials and supplies?

• How frequently do minor accidents occur in the classroom? Do children stumble over chairs? Do bookcases and shelves sometimes tip over? Do constructions get knocked over by traffic wandering through the block area? And do children frequently collide because the placement of furniture encourages running in the classroom?

• Is the environment too stimulating in places? Do children flit from one activity to another because the arrangement is not conducive to concentrating on tasks?

• Does the spatial arrangement encourage shouting and boisterous behavior and does the teacher constantly remind children to use their "inside voices."?

• Is the physical organization of space such that the teacher is free to observe and interact with children? Or is the teacher's time consumed by maintenance tasks like mopping up drips and spills or picking up coats and other belongings?

• Are routines consistent, transitions smooth, and clean-up time organized so that children assist in putting away materials and keeping the environment orderly, or does the teacher end up doing the bulk of the tidying up?

Exercise 29
Pinpointing my problem areas

When children are pummeling one another over the head with a disputed toy, the best short-run solution is to separate the combatants and try to restore a semblance of peace. But the only way to guarantee long-term tranquility is to change the conditions that created the conflict. This means taking a hard look at the spatial arrangement to determine how it is affecting classroom management.

In the space below, list the spatial and organizational problems that you see in your own center. You may have problem areas that you are already aware of either in your classroom or administrative support space. Write these down, and add to your list as you read further in this chapter.

Next to each problem area, pinpoint the restrictions that may presently be keeping you from resolving your problem. These could be time constraints, money restrictions, or simply finding the opportunity to discuss and work out the problem with others with whom you share the space.

	Problem	*Constraints*
1.		
2.		
3.		
4.		
5.		
6.		
7.		
8.		
9.		
10.		

Blueprint for Change—The Critical Dimensions

Bringing together the elements of successful spatial arrangements in an early childhood setting takes time and thoughtful analysis. We have begun that process by assessing our use of space in our own work environments. Now we look at the critical dimensions for evaluating space. This means defining the factors that play a vital role in determining whether or not our use of space is in harmony with our stated objectives. The critical dimensions include:

- light
- color
- texture
- sound
- temperature and ventilation
- size and shape

Individual circumstances will vary on how much control directors and teachers have for determining the extent to which these factors can be adjusted within any given environment. Obviously, those educators involved in designing and renovating centers will be able to exercise wider discretion. Individuals coping with existing space contraints may be able to modify their setting only slightly. An awareness of the principles, however, will provide a useful framework for all workers to analyze their early childhood setting.[7]

Lighting

Research on the effects of light on the physiology of humans and animals indicates that lighting may be a powerful influence on the attention span and behavior of children.[8] Many teachers have found, for instance that toning down lighting by manual dimmer controls helps calm children. Others keep the lights off altogether if natural light sources are sufficient. This not only produces a calming effect on the classroom, it also saves electricity.

Careful attention to lighting is critical in the early childhood center because of the amount of time spent on visual tasks. A general rule is to use lower illumination levels for activities that are less active and require concentration and higher illumination for more active areas that do not require as much concentration. In assessing the lighting needs of a school environment there are four types of lighting sources commonly used: natural, fluorescent, incandescent, and high-intensity discharge lamps. The type of lighting selected must be tailored to the type of activity going on within a specific area.

Flexibility is most important. Mobile track units that hold fixtures, separate dimmer switches, and movable sources are the most versatile for classroom use, allowing workers to create "pools of light" where needed. Center needs range from totally dark environments for showing a movie or filmstrip, dimness for nap or rest time, to good illumination for most other activities.

Natural light is the most economical but also the most unpredictable source of lighting. Windows can make a small room appear larger by making the outdoors an extension of the indoor environment. Roof overhangs, shades, and blinds can be used to control natural light and adjust for unwanted glare. Skylights also provide an additional source of natural light and contribute to energy-wise heating and cooling of the building.

Windows should be approximately one-fifth of the floor space area, and roughly one-half of them should be openable. Window-sills 22"–24" high allow children to see out and bring the outdoors in. This can have a calming effect on children if there is an abundance of green foliage within view.

Diffused light from fluorescent bulbs housed in plastic panels is good for use with young children because it provides well-distributed light with little heat. Fluorescent lighting is far less expensive to operate than incandescent lighting though more expensive initially. Overall, it may be three to four times more efficient and require less replacement and maintenance.[9] The best shades of fluorescent light to use are the warm tones like "deluxe/warm white," (similar to light emitted by incandescent lights) or "vita lite" (similar to light emitted by the sun).[10]

Color

Color is perhaps the single most powerful visual cue that attracts young children in their environments. Studies indicate that color perception dominates over form perception in small children. Inappropriate color may actually produce unintended behavior. Therefore, the ways we use color in early childhood settings have a strong influence on the behavior of children and on our classroom management. But color also affects adults in the school environment, so color as a design tool must be approached in an integrated, well-thought-out manner.

In selecting colors, it is useful to remember that the orange-red-yellow "warm" tones of the color spectrum tend to stimulate. The blue-green-purple "cool" hues, on the other hand, tend to calm. If we employ these guidelines to classroom activity areas, we will use the warm tones in high activity areas and reserve the cool shades for napping, reading and areas where we desire concentration and quiet behavior.

Henner Ertel believes that colors may have a decisive influence on the child's mental performance as well.[11] His studies have found that the proper selection of colors can have an impact on the child's IQ. Certain colors like blue, yellow, yellow-green, or orange stimulate alertness and creativity while white, black, and brown playrooms make children duller.

Maria Montessori emphasized in her Children's House that the environment should not detract from the serious work of the child. She describes her classrooms as having bland, light-colored walls and shelves that contrasted with the colorful materials. She felt that the purpose of color was to reduce the extraneous stimuli and direct the child to specific parts of the learning environment.

Colors may be utilized in the school environment to make spaces take on different characteristics. For example, light colors tend to make rooms appear larger, darker colors make rooms look smaller. Cool colors stress the room's vertical elements, making the ceiling appear higher. Mildly contrasting colors can be an effective way to separate workspaces. For large background areas and walls used to display artwork, posters and graphics, neutral colors like white, cream, or pale gray are good. However, light colors show spots and handprints so an easily cleaned finish is essential. Many designers have also used color graphics on the walls and floors to serve as a guide for children to appropriate activities. To be effective, though, color cues should be low enough for children to see at their level.

There is a critical link between color and light that must also be considered. Color depends on light in order to be seen. And, depending on the warmness or coolness of the light source or whether the source is artificial or natural, the results may be strikingly different.[12] For example, red shades look excellent under warm white incandescent light, while blue tones look good under natural light or cool-white fluorescent lighting.

The colors used in a room are also important for determining the effectiveness of the lighting. Light-colored ceilings, walls, and floor surfaces are good for reflecting light and distributing it evenly throughout the environment. Depending on the natural light filtering into a building, colors may play an important role in the psychological effects of "cooling" or "warming" an area. In general, light shades of green or soft pastels are good for walls with a southern or western exposure. Rooms with a northern exposure may need a shade of yellow or a strong light-reflecting color.[13]

Texture

It has been said that much of Frank Lloyd Wright's success was due to his understanding that people need to "experience" space, that the more senses people use in their environment, the more aesthetically interesting that environment will be. In keeping with this architectural philosophy, Wright was a master at using texture in his buildings. Alternating between rough and smooth and degrees in between, he created tactile-rich environments for people to live and work in. It is unfortunate that designers of child care environments have not embraced Wright's philosophy and given more attention to creating tactile wonderlands for children. Even more than adults, children rely upon their sense of touch to explore, discover, and learn about the world.

There are many things that we can do, however, to increase our use of texture within our individual child care settings. Most important is to emphasize "soft" surroundings to counter the institution-like "hard" surroundings present in most buildings.[14] Softness is introduced into the environment through objects that give tactile stimulation and invite us to touch. Indoors this might mean rugs, pillows, cushions, a rocker, or a chair to snuggle up on. It also means a variety of materials that are easily malleable, like clay, play dough, finger paints, and sand. Outdoor softness is available through water, sand, mud, and dirt, plus lots of grass to roll around on.

Textures can also help cue children to appropriate activities for particular areas. Soft environments are good for low-activity areas; hard surfaces (tile, wood, asphalt) encourage louder, more active participation. Keying activities appropriately helps with managing the space over-all.

Adults, too, need a variety of textures in their environment. Carpeting, an easy chair, and texturally interesting wall coverings and floor materials can provide tactile variety for adult work spaces in our centers.

Sound

It will come as no surprise to child care workers that noise is tiring, over an extended period leading to nervousness, irritability, and inefficiency. One trainee, asked how she liked her new job, replied that the most important prerequisite for working in early childhood education was not asked at her job interview nor ever discussed in college coursework. In fact, she went on to say, that it

had nothing at all to do with her knowledge of child development, curriculum methods, and teaching techniques. What it boiled down to was stamina—her threshold tolerance for noise and commotion!

This may be an overstatement, but the fact remains that noise is a critical factor in the stress that many child care workers attribute to their jobs. But a certain amount of noise is inevitable whenever a group of children get together. What we need to do is channel this "verbal energy" into constructive outlets, and use space effectively to minimize its negative impact on us.

Excessive noise can be particularly troublesome in trying to do administrative tasks. Typing, talking on the telephone, or conducting business with parents and visitors needs to be done as far away from the children's activities as possible. Otherwise a cycle develops where voices are raised to be heard over the din contributing to the decibel level and causing everyone to raise their voices even higher. Furthermore, a caller inquiring about the program can get a poor first impression when a racket can be heard filtering through the receiver.

Some considerations: Long rectangular rooms are more difficult for acoustical control than square rooms. Hardwood, tile, and linoleum floors can cause more noise than rooms with carpeting or even scattered area rugs. Drapes, wall hangings, padding on furniture, tableclothes, and room dividers all contribute to acoustical control. Even wall finishes of soft, porous materials (for example, soft pine) may be helpful in deadening sound.

High ceilings can be treated with acoustical absorption tiles, or by suspending billowing parachutes and banners to help decrease the decibel level. However, acoustical absorption materials underfoot are more effective and more economical than acoustical materials overhead. Either floor or ceiling should be treated, but not both because this produces a deadening effect.

The best acoustical control comes from planning activities so that the quieter ones are clustered together and the more boisterous activities are likewise grouped together. Some teachers have also found that soft background music calms voices. Combating noise with noise sounds illogical, but it works.

Temperature and ventilation

High temperatures can cause fatigue, as anyone who has worked in a hot, stuffy room over a period of time can testify. But cold, drafty environments are also not pleasant to work in. Finding a comfortable temperature is no easy task, though. We all differ in our internal comfort zones. Putting workers together in one facility is no guarantee that they will be compatible in what feels appropriate and comfortable.

With an eye on saving energy as well as reducing utility costs, it is best to keep room temperatures between 68 and 72 degrees. Because young children in a child care setting do many of their activities on the floor, consideration must also be given to floor temperature. Radiant heating keeps floors warm and free from drafts, but can have fatiguing effect if not well regulated. For comfort, the humidity level in the classroom should be in the 50 to 75 percent range. An open aquarium or exposed water table will add humidity to the air if the climate is dry.

Also, it is important not to neglect good ventilation. Good ventilation means delivering enough oxygen to keep the body and brain alert. Sufficient ventilation is also necessary to reduce odors from the restroom area, from cleaning disinfectants, or from bug and plant sprays. In a school, unpleasant odors may have a particularly strong impact on first-time visitors. Conversely, pleasant aromas can create a positive influence on behavior and our over-all feelings about the environment. One parent visiting a program told the director that as soon as she walked into the reception area, the aroma of fresh bread wafting from the school's kitchen convinced her that her daughter must attend that center. She said that any place that created such delicious smells would probably also give her child a lot of love and attention.

Size and shape

Another environmental factor that plays an important role in the early childhood setting is the size and shape of the space that adults and children occupy. This affects us in two ways. First, there is the psychological impact that the size and shape of the room or building has on us directly. Second, there is the relation of that size and shape to the number of people using it.

Most people, adults and children alike, feel overwhelmed by large, undifferentiated spaces. Recall the last time you visited a huge auditorium, exhibit hall, or Grand Central Station. The way we feel in large rooms, particularly those with soaring ceilings, can directly affect how we use that space and how secure we feel. Similarly, small rooms or odd-shaped rooms can also have either a positive or negative impact on our behavior depending on how the space is utilized. Long narrow rooms in particular seem to affect the behavior of young children beckoning them to run down the corridor-like space. Likewise, square rooms usually have activity centers placed around the walls, thus leaving a dead space in the middle of the room that creates classroom management problems.

Some educators feel that rooms with a ceiling height of 7 to 8 feet make the teacher appear excessively large to the children. Many architects recommend a ceiling height of 10 to 11 feet for spaces shared by both adults and children, with additional spaces with 4-foot ceiling heights designed exclusively for child use to create a sense of intimacy for the children.[15]

It is also important to consider the number of people that occupy a given area. Research has correlated the relation between the amount of space and negative or aggressive behavior in people.[16] But child care workers already know that children crowded together get restless and engage in socially unacceptable behavior. What studies have been helpful in showing, however, is the correlation between density (the number of children within a given space) and the degree of restlessness, inattention and negative behavior. The best social involvement seems to occur at a medium density, 35–50-square feet of space per child. When there is too little space and consequently a high density, less than 35-square feet per child, children engage in more acts of aggressive behavior. But it is possible to have too much space. When the density is too low, more than 50-square feet per child, children wander aimlessly supervision is poorer, and accidents happen.

On the other hand, when crowded conditions occur in a predictable pattern, both adults and children seem to handle the situation better. For example, we get more upset at a traffic jam that occurs at midday than as anticipated at rush hour. In our centers, we know that congestion will occur around the entry and dismissal times and we can handle it. But when our environment gets congested at other times, it is more difficult for us to deal with.

Space in any child care setting can be divided into three categories, all three of which must be sufficient to insure program quality. First there is the *children's activity space.* Most state licensing agencies set standards for compliance that are roughly 35-square feet per child. This is the space designated for the children's daily activities in the classroom. It does not include storage, napping, restroom, or circulation space. Unless a program has a free-flow schedule and utilizes outdoor areas throughout the day, this 35-square-feet-per-child guideline is an absolute minimum. Programs should strive to provide 40–45-square feet per child and even 50-square feet when space is ample.

Support space includes areas designated for food preparation, storage, cubbies, lockers, napping, and toileting as well as all administrative and teacher preparation space. This is the area of space allocation that most often gets shortchanged because it is not held to standards by the state licensing agencies. But it is this category of space that most directly affects teacher and administrative effectiveness. Too many centers skimp on teacher prep space in particular and expect these functions somehow to get done in the general classroom space. When storage is inadequate, when administrative functions are conducted in the children's space, and when teachers have no place to retreat, the entire program suffers. Programs should strive for roughly 30–40-square feet per child for this support space category.

The third area of space in a center is termed *nonuseable space*. This includes space taken up by walls, partitions, circulation, and mechanical maintenance fixtures like the heating and cooling system. In quality programs, this space generally takes up approximately 18–25-square feet per child.

When all categories are added together, we see that quality programs allocate roughly 88–115-square feet per child attending at any one time.[17] The evidence is straightforward: Programs that value the spatial needs of children and adults allocate adequate space for the functions necessary to run a quality program.

Organizing Classroom Space

In most teacher-training institutions, little time is devoted to the importance of the physical environment in the classroom as an integral part of the learning experience for children. They emphasize curriculum methods and materials, theories of instruction, and philosophies of education, yet one of the most influential teaching "tools"—the physical setting—is neglected.

The way we organize our classroom environments says a lot to children about how we feel about them, how we think they learn, and how we expect them to learn. In many respects, our arrangement of space serves as a kind of *hidden curriculum*, relaying powerful messages to children about our expectations for their behavior.

In many subtle, nonverbal ways, the environment communicates our expectations. It is a potent force in shaping children's behavior and achieving our professional objectives. Too often, however, the spatial arrangement works at cross purposes with our stated objectives. We say, for example, that one of our classroom goals is to teach self-reliance and instill a sense of initiative in children. But if materials are stored out of reach and children have to rely on us to get things for them, they are clearly getting mixed messages. Likewise, if we remind children to walk but have situated the furniture to encourage running, our nonverbal signals will speak louder than our words. It is vital, then, that the organization of space within our classroom flows out of our philosophy and directly relates to the goals we pursue. If it doesn't, frustration is bound to result.

Our task in organizing classroom space is to assess our educational philosophy and implement specific design patterns consistant with that philosophy. If we believe, for instance, that the children learn from one another and want to encourage and exchange of information between children, we can organize the classroom environment to achieve that objective. We can structure the setting to accommodate small group activities, use round tables that encourage social interaction and communication, and set up specific activities and projects that require two children to work together (like a teeter-totter or a pulley-and-lever activity). Or we can specifically design an activity area that conveys to children that we expect them to help one another. One school, for example, has a small board with the words "I can tie shoes. Can I tie yours?" The names and pictures of children that have qualified for this special status are displayed below. Another center has designated a special rocking chair in the library corner for older children to use to read to the younger ones.

In projecting how philosophy and goals can be translated into concrete spatial patterns, it is useful to think of a continuum of formality and structure. Then we can assess where we as individuals (or as a group of teachers sharing the same space) fit into that continuum. On the one end is a highly structured teacher-directed model. This embraces the idea that the teacher is the source of knowledge, and that the spatial arrangement should facilitate teacher-directed instruction. This environment would probably want a minimum of distractions. The teacher would be accessible and have good supervision of the classroom at all times. At the other end of the spectrum is the informal, open model with a philosophy that holds that children are the source of their own knowledge. Such an environment would encourage free choice and provide a variety of activity centers where children could discover and learn for themselves.

Recognition of one's own place on this continuum is most essential if we want to tailor our classroom arrangement to flow out of our philosophy and be consistent with our goals. This is not to imply a static situation, however. Quite the contrary. As we grow professionally and broaden our awareness about teaching and learning methods, we should also adapt the physical setting in our classrooms to reflect our new awareness and continue to support our goals.

The elements of a good early childhood environment

Even given the wide range of educational philosophies, there are fundamental elements that most early childhod educators agree contribute to good environments for young children. These elements evolve out of the developmental needs of children—physical, intellectual, and social-emotional. As such, they form the foundation for implementing the specific design patterns that we will discuss later in this chapter.

Children need an environment that is friendly and safe: For many children, attending a child care center is the first separation from their parents on a regular basis. This experience is anxiety-

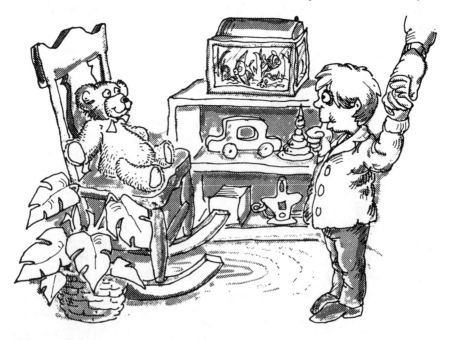

provoking for some children and equally traumatic for some parents! It is obviously to our own interest as well as theirs to do as much as we can to create an environment that makes the transition from home to school as non-threatening as possible.

The entry or reception area of the classroom is particularly important for a smooth transition. This area should provide a link with the familiar surrounding of the child's home. Plants, comfortable furniture, an aquarium, a small rocker, and a stuffed animal or two along with calm colors and inviting smiles all communicate warmth and acceptance. If possible, the entry area should be situated out of the mainstream of activity so the new child will not feel bombarded by the commotion and can take time to make a slow adjustment if necessary.

Some designers suggest that the pathway leading to the center is important for conveying a sense of care, concern, and friendliness to the child. Glimpses into the front courtyard can help the transition. And if the scale of the building is homelike and an institutional atmosphere avoided, the child will more readily accept the new surroundings.

Children more easily adjust to a new center if they also feel that it is safe and secure. Furnishings should be stable and not tip over easily, stairs should be easily negotiable, and corners on furniture should be rounded if possible. Shatterproof glass, thermostatically controlled hot water, and shockproof electrical outlets are also essential for a safe environment for children. It is only common sense to take steps to insure that medical and toxic cleaning supplies are locked out of the reach of children. Finally, we also need to insure that our playground climbing structures are splinter-free and do not have hazardous sharp edges or protrusions.

Children need an environment scaled to their developmental needs: Even the doors, fixtures, and furnishings can motivate the child's curiosity and become a valuable learning experience. Creating a child-size environment that is stimulating and functional can pay extra dividends as well. A classroom scaled to children's developmental needs capitalizes on their emerging sense of independence, and helps them take more responsibility for caring for their own environment. The child care worker can then spend less time in maintenance-related tasks and devote that time to more personally rewarding interactions with the children.

Child-size drinking fountains, windows, sinks, clocks, thermometers, tables, chairs, and storage units can all contribute to creating a feeling in the child that "This is the place where I am not totally dependent on adults." In an environment scaled for young children, they can reach hardware, latches, and doorknobs. Railings and handles are small enough for their hands to grip. Child-size fixtures in the bathroom also promote self-sufficiency. Scaling the environment to meet the needs of small children also helps them compensate for poor motor coordination and slow reaction time. On the other hand, independence must be balanced with safety, so doors, cupboards, and other parts of the classroom not intended for the use of children should have adult-height knobs or other safety features.

There are many things we can do as teachers to help children develop a sense of independence. In one respect our task is easy, because children are eager to learn to take care of themselves. All we need to do is tailor the environment to facilitate that growing sense of autonomy. But children will not internalize a sense of order unless they are in an orderly environment. If we want them to help, we need to structure the environment in ways that help them become helpful.

One of the things we can do is to reinforce consistency both in daily routines and in the location of activities and materials. If children know each day what to expect, they can anticipate and feel more secure, and thus internalize a sense of responsibility for their own actions.

One area of the classroom where we can help children take this initiative is in the cubby/locker area. Cubbies are a convenient way to help children learn to care for their personal belongings. It is important, however, that the cubby/locker area be situated in such a way that a child can take time to attend to personal-care tasks. Low hooks, easy-to-reach storage trays, and a low bench that the child can sit on to put on boots, coats, and other garments without being in the way of traffic is one way to help children achieve a sense of autonomy.

The possibilities for cubbies are many. Milk crates, plastic trays, 5-gallon ice-cream tubs, sturdy cardboard boxes, or built-in partitions are some of the cubby systems that centers use. Each cubby should be personalized to indicate ownership. The child's name, a photograph, and perhaps some kind of personalized decoration help children identify which cubby is theirs. They can thus become responsible for putting away their lunch, art work, and other assorted treasures throughout the day. Some schools have found it helpful to color-code cubbies or match them up with a colored tote bag that the child can cart home each day.

Other daily routines like watering the plants or caring for the animals also help instill a sense of responsibility. When children can assist in this way, they generally also become more concerned about the welfare of living things and treat them with greater respect.

Locating items in consistent places is another way to help children become more self-sufficient. The display and storage of materials and equipment must be simple and uncluttered to facilitate easy clean-up. Labeling shelves or using photographs, pictures, or contact-paper cutouts of the item all contribute to helping children return materials to their proper location.

Picture sequence cards can also be used to foster independence. A sequence card display of how to operate a cassette tape record, a record player, or other equipment means less time that the teacher has to spend assisting in these tasks.

Children need an environment that enhances their feelings of self-esteem: A positive self-image is at the heart of learning and motivation in the early years. And there are many things we can do through the arrangement of space and materials that conveys the powerful message that we value our students' presence in our classroom. Many of the things we have already discussed, like creating a friendly homelike atmosphere and a child-sized environment, also promote feelings of positive self-esteem. But there are many other ways that we can arrange our classroom environments to let children know that we respect and care for them as individuals.

Children love to see themselves in photographs. We can capitalize on this by creating wall displays depicting different activities they have done in the classroom or on field trips they have taken. Annual scrapbooks can be compiled from these photographs and added to the children's library. Many teachers have developed a weekly rotating "You Are Special" display which highlights an individual student each week. When these classroom displays reflect the cultural diversity and ethnic heritage of our students, they also convey the important message that each child is a valued member of the group.

Children can develop a sense of belonging when they take part in a daily "Helping Hands" planning board, or attach their name tag to a peg board headed, "I Am Here Today!" Displaying children's artwork throughout the room and having them take an active role in assembling bulletin boards and arranging classroom furniture also helps communicate that their hard work is valued and their opinions appreciated.

An environment that values the individual needs of children respects the child's need for solitary work spaces. Often in our eagerness to cultivate a sense of community, we overlook the fact that children also need time to be alone. Young children need space where they can explore freely but they also need places to stand back, pause, and just observe. These can be a secluded nook or cranny of the classroom, or a window seat or rocking horse in a quiet corner of the room. We should also try to create child-size caves and cozy places for one or two children to hide in. These needn't be elaborate. Boxes, crates, tables, tentlike structures, large cement pipes, or a child-size loft can make special places for children to retreat to. We can make these private spaces extra special by incorporating a small shell collection to study, a terrarium to look at, or a cozy cushion and a couple of books to browse through.

One final way we can enhance feelings of self-esteem is to place mirrors strategically throughout our classroom. Small mirrors, large mirrors, mirrors on the ceiling, mirrors on the floor, mirrors in child-size caves, concave mirrors, distorting mirrors, and mirrors with assorted messages like "wink," "smile," or "we love you!" will surely be favorites of the children.

Guidelines for implementing design patterns

The way we define areas in our early childhood environments through the layout of furniture and materials has a direct bearing on the success of our program. A well-organized classroom cuts down on wasted motion, reduces confusion, and markedly influences behavior of our students.[18]

A good layout begins with considering the types of activity that we want to go on in our classroom and how they interrelate. By structuring their placement to channel traffic from one area to another, we can reduce congestion, eliminate empty dead space, and avoid overused space. In the process, we facilitate involvement in activities by eliminating interruptions and intrusions into activity areas.

Delineating space can be achieved through the use of movable partitions, low bookcases, storage shelves, and movable furniture like pianos and tables. By using these items in conjunction with permanent dividers and walls, we can create varying degrees of enclosure, insuring that activities have the necessary visual and auditory separation. But we need not limit ourselves to movable units to achieve spatial separation of activities. Platforms, pits, lofts and balconies or changes in color, lighting, and wall graphics can also define use and delineate space.

There is no precise formula to follow to decide how much classroom space should be kept open and how much should be taken up by tables, shelves and other pieces of equipment and furniture. Some researchers suggest that if more than two-thirds of the surface is covered, too little room is left to maneuver in; but if less than one-half of the surface is covered, too much open space is left.[19]

The key to effective layout of space is flexibility. The early childhood program requires that space and equipment be easily adaptable to permit activities to expand, shrink or disappear completely as the classroom needs change. Changing the environment periodically may also lead to more exploring and greater involvement with materials and equipment. It is important, therefore, that all furniture be as mobile and easy to store as possible.

Implementing design patterns in the classroom is not a haphazard exercise. To determine effectively the placement of each activity, teachers can manipulate scaled-down pieces of paper cut-outs on a large sheet of graph paper on which the permanent structures in the classroom are outlined. In this way we can see the flow from one activity center to another and experiment with all the possibilities. In doing so, we need to ask ourselves the following questions about each activity we plan to include in our program:

- What group size is most appropriate for the activity?
- How much concentration does the activity require?
- What kind of supervision does the activity require?
- What are the storage and display needs of the activity?
- What kind of maintenance and clean-up does the activity entail?
- What water or electrical restrictions does the activity impose?
- What activities might be moved outdoors?

What group size is most appropriate for the activity? Successful classroom management in large part rests on our ability to determine the appropriate group size for the activity centers we have planned and to arrange the space to accommodate that group size. Determining the best group size for an activity center will come from consideration of the following:

- The objective of the activity—if we want children to learn to take turns and share at a water table, we will probably want to limit the group size to two to four children.
- The amount of supplies and materials we have for the activity—if we only have four pair of scissors, we would be inviting trouble if we arranged an art activity space for more than four to five children.
- The size and amount of furniture we have for the activity—if only six chairs can comfortably fit around a table, we would obviously want to limit that activity to six children.

• The mobility required for the activity—if the activity is a passive one like a group story time, the size of the group might be different than an activity requiring high mobility like dance or gymnastics.

One of the features of a well-designed classroom is that the learning centers are structured to accommodate a variety of different group sizes. These include spaces for:

• Solitary play—a listening post, a rocking horse, a cozy cave, or a book alcove.

• two to four children—an easel, sandbox, water table, or woodworking bench.

• five to eight children—an art activity table, dramatic play corner, a small group music or movement class, or story-time.

• eight or more children—a puppet show presentation, movie, naptime, or a circle-time group experience.

These groupings will vary from classroom to classroom, of course, depending on the teacher's curriculum objectives, the amount and variety of materials available, and the physical size and shape of the room.

How much concentration does the activity require? In general, the less distractibility desired, the greater the sense of enclosure necessary to provide visual and auditory separation from other activities. Sometimes this separation can be achieved with earphones or by merely directing the seating or angle of the table so that the focus of attention is in a direction with no distractions.

At other times, however, it may be necessary to create specific boundaries by using shelves or bookcases. This is particularly important for activities like block play. Children will not feel free to engage in creative block-building if their structures are in jeopardy of being knocked over by passing traffic.

Most centers have found that a two-foot-high divider is sufficient to create a sense of enclosure for a floor activity. A three-foot-high divider is appropriate for sitting activities, and a four-foot divider necessary for standing activities.

What kind of supervision does the activity require? In a classroom with dividers no higher than four feet, a teacher standing can usually have fairly good supervision of the activities going on. But the teacher's time is valuable. To the extent we can locate in the teacher's sphere of vision, activities that need more supervision (particularly those involving potentially dangerous equipment like scissors or expensive equipment like tape recorders and record players), we can cut down on unnecessary running back and forth.

Some activities like a cooking project will require constant supervision and involvement by the teacher. It may be helpful to locate these activities adjacent to activities that require minimal supervision so that a teacher covering a specific part of the classroom will not have to supervise too much.

What are the storage and display needs of the activity? The guiding principle for storage of supplies and materials is to locate them as close as possible to the work surface for that activity. The storage shelf for puzzles, for example, should be directly adjacent to where we expect the child to put the puzzle together. This eliminates the possibility that the child will be bumped, stumble, or fall with puzzle in hand enroute to the activity table. It also facilitates clean-up by children when putting the item back on the appropriate shelf means only one or two steps instead of a dozen or more.

This principle is crucial when we consider the art area in our classrooms. We want to avoid having children walk across a circulation path with scissors, paint, or other materials that would have disasterous consequences if a collision occurred.

What kind of maintenance and clean-up does the activity entail? All floors, walls, and activity work surfaces must be both functional and durable in our early childhood classrooms. That means simply, easy to clean! If we are trying to decide where to locate an activity center for potentially messy art projects, we will want to locate it on the most easy-to-clean floor surface (one with a floor drain, if possible). We will also want to situate it as close to a water source for both art prep and for clean-up. Moreover, we should locate it as close as possible to the drying racks or area where completed projects will be located. Handy paper-towel dispensers and convenient mop and a sponge bucket close at hand to the art work surface prepare us for the inevitable drips and spills that accompany art endeavors.

Other activity areas like the cooking center, the water table, or the animal and nature study area should also be located in areas that facilitate easy access to water.

What electrical restrictions does the activity impose? Many teachers find that electrical restrictions often dictate where their activity centers are located. If we are planning a music and movement activity that incorporates a record player, for example, we may be limited to locating it next to whatever electrical outlets we already have in the classroom. Likewise a tape-recorder listening station, a cooking center, or an area designated for viewing filmstrips or movies must be in close proximity to electrical outlets. A safety tip: If using an extension cord is unavoidable, play it safe. Dangling cords that are easy to trip over invite accidents. Tape the extension cord to the floor while in use, then remove as soon as the activity has been completed.

What activities might be moved outdoors? When we think "classroom," we should automatically view the outdoors as an extension of our indoor learning environments and encourage a free flow between the outside and inside space if possible. Outdoor activities are an integral part of learning, providing adventure, challenge and a full range of learning experiences.

We should view outdoor environments as a way to relieve some of the space constraints that we experience indoors. Nature studies, woodworking, messy art activities, obstacle courses, and perceptual-motor activities are some of the activities that we can successfully extend outdoors. In fact, a covered courtyard, porch, or deck with indoor-outdoor carpeting is a good solution to cramped quarters and can open up space for a wide variety of year-around activities.

Remember, however, that the same principles of delineating space also apply to outdoors. If we want our activity centers fo flow out of our philosophy and achieve our program objectives, the same thoughtful analysis of space requirements should precede the layout of outdoor space. Only in this way will we be guaranteed a successful total learning environment.

Exercise 30
My activity inventory

Now comes the opportunity for you to take the general design principles discussed and apply them to your specific classroom. Every setting is unique in its size, shape, and range and variety of materials available. The only way you will get a first-hand appreciation of all the spatial requirements of your program is to detail the important elements for each and then look at how they overlap and relate to one another.

What we find by doing this analysis is that no activity center operates in isolation. It is the interplay between all activities in the classroom that determines the success of the spatial arrangement.

Using the following chart as your worksheet, fill in the information as it relates to your specific program. Select the first activity that you want to analyze. Some possibilities might include:

- music and rhythms
- woodworking/carpentry
- art (messy)
- art (not-so-messy)
- dramatic play house
- nature study—plants & animals
- sand play
- water play
- language arts/reading readiness
- manipulative games/puzzles
- practical life/sensorial materials
- library corner
- cubby/locker
- snack/cooking projects
- nap/rest area
- unit blockbuilding
- large hollow-block building
- listening post (tape or records)

- mathematical concepts
- science exploration & discovery center
- perceptual-motor activities
- flannel board/chalk board activities

Now proceed across the page for each activity and fill in the remaining columns. Don't worry at this point about any apparent conflicts. Once the chart is completed, you will see that many of the activities will have to share space or in some way overlap with others. The purpose of this inventory is to determine compatibility and see how the many strands can be woven together into a well-developed spatial pattern.

ACTIVITY INVENTORY

Name of activity	Group size	Concentration level required	Noise level of activity	Maintenance & clean-up	Storage/Display required	Special restrictions (water, electrical, light)

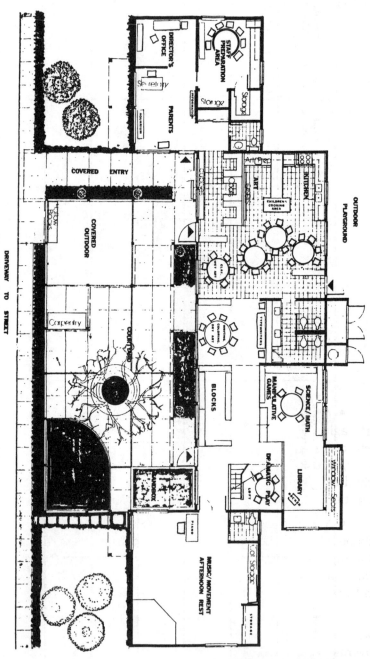

Sample Floor Plan—CREATIVE LEARNING CENTER, Alamo, CA

Architect: Richard Sharpiro
Berkeley, California

A Potpourri of Organizing Tips for the Classroom

• *Can't keep track of felt-tipped marking pens?* Attach a long string onto the end of a marking pen and loop to form a necklace. When teachers or parent participants arrive in the morning they can put on their felt-tipped necklace. They will never have to scurry about looking for a marker when they need to write a child's name on a paper during the course of the day.

• *Musical instruments are fragile:* Don't run the risk of damaging musical instruments by heaping them into a box at the end of a rhythms session. Outline the shapes of the tambourines, bells, shakers, and other instruments onto a large peg board. The children can then be responsible for returning them to their proper location. The same can be done for kitchen utensils or art supplies.

• *Make clean-up a learning experience:* Outline the geometric shapes of unit blocks onto the storage shelves where they are kept. Children will more readily clean up blocks because they'll enjoy the challenge of classifying shapes as they put the blocks away. Incidentally, varnishing blocks will make them last longer.

• *If noise is a real problem:* Cover the woodworking bench with a low-pile carpet to help deaden the sound and lower the overall noise level. Carpet pieces can also be applied to storage shelves.

• *Short on space for a garden?* Ask your neighborhood service station for a couple of old tires. Put the tires on your porch, deck, or an out-of-the way spot in the playground. Fill with soil and plant with seedlings. Perfect for yards where gophers are tenants.

• *Consider the vertical growing space in your classroom:* Make a lush screen of foliage by stringing wire or cord from a bookcase, shelf or piano top up to the ceiling. Start several sweet potato plants and attach the young vines to the string. By the end of the year you'll have a beautiful green divider. Southern exposure is best for your horticultural experiment.

• *Can't afford an elaborate woodworking bench?* Call your local tree surgeon and ask for a large slice from a tree being cut down (roughly 2′ high and 1′ wide). Pound several dozen nails into the top so they are just secure. Children will enjoy wielding a hammer to complete the pounding task.

• *Create a king-sized geo-board:* Ask your lumber yard for a piece of ¾" plywood about 4″ × 3″. Drill holes into the plywood at 3″ intervals. Secure pieces of ½" dowel into the holes with white glue. Let dry and paint. Now cut several pieces from an old inner tube from a bicycle tire. These can then be stretched like large rubber bands to make interesting geometric shapes on your king-sized geo-board.

• *Chalkboards need not be elaborate:* You can create several inexpensive chalkboards for indoor or outdoor use at your center by using a jigsaw to carve out various shapes out of ¼″ Masonite. Hardware stores sell chalkboard paint that can then be brushed on (several coats) and sanded to a smooth finish.

• *Have problems with sand being tracked into your classroom from the playground?* Construct a sandscraper that children will love to use. Pound together three floor brushes so that the bristles are facing inward in the shape of a U. Children can place their sandy shoe in the scraper to brush off loose sand. You might also want to develop a playground checkout board to help keep track of sand-scooping shovels and supplies. Attach a small chalk board to a peg board where scoops and shovels can be checked out (and returned) by having children write their name (or name-scribble) on the chalkboard before checking out equipment.

• *Housepainting can be fun:* Children will delight in "painting" the building. All you need is a plastic bucket, a large brush, and lots of water. But how do you keep track of the brushes and prevent them from getting lost? Just drill a small hole in the handle and attach a long string. Attach the other end of the string to the bucket handle.

• *Nonverbal cues can save our lungs:* Tired of having to regulate the number of children at certain activities for fear that conflicts will occur because of overcrowding? Let the children regulate themselves. Post a large numeral next to the activity indicating the desired number that should use that activity. (A good counting experience besides.) This method works well for a small loft area, for a water table, or a block area that has a limited number of blocks. Or, how about using signs to indicate when an area is off limits? Children will enjoy deciphering your messages.

Water play for two: A galvanized tub can serve as the perfect water play set up for two children. It's easy to empty and move about as well. Equip with a variety of funnels, strainers, tubes, and plastic bottles and your twosome will be occupied for hours. Make the experience even more interesting by adding a drop or two of food coloring to the water and several capfuls of dishwashing soap.

• *Can't find a suitable drying rack for your student's master-pieces?* Try hanging a large fish net on the wall above the easel painting area. When children complete a painting, it can be secured to the net with two clothespins.

• *Junkyards are marvelous for digging up treasures:* For example, search out an old television set. Leave the insides behind and take home the cabinet and paint a bright color. Attach a curtain and you've got a perfect puppet theater.

• *Do you have trouble keeping your cassette tapes and storybooks matched up?* Buy a box of the large ziplock storage bags. Attach heavy yarn to the top of the bag to form a handle. Now you have the perfect storage bag for your storybook and tape combos.

• *Are you equipped for "who knows what" on field trips?* Carry along a large lunch box with a few emergency items that are often needed on field trips: a can opener, pencil, pad of paper, paper clips, mirror, small scissors, business cards, roll of dimes, matches, post cards and a few stamps, return address stickers, flashlight, screwdriver, flares, paper cups, clean wipes, and of course, a first aid kit.

• *Do your magic markers dry up because the tops get misplaced?* Here's a permanent solution. Pour 1" to 2" of plaster of paris into a small 6" aluminum pie plate. When partially set, place the caps to the markers in the plaster of paris so that the holes are visible. Let completely dry and take out of the aluminum plate. Place the markers into the caps securely.

Organizing Support Space for Administration and Teacher Prep

Our immediate physical surroundings play a compelling role in our motivation, productivity, and interpersonal relationships on the job. If we are serious about creating an atmosphere that counters the potentially stressful effects inherent in child care responsibilities, we must address the spatial needs of people working together for eight or more hours a day. Educators focusing their attention on the needs of children in the child care setting too often neglect their own needs. Sufficient, well-organized support space is vital for maintaining high morale among staff.

The key to providing well-organized support space is flexibility. It must accommodate a wide variety of activities as well as being friendly, warm and inviting. Because the support needs of the school environment are so diverse, organizing adult work spaces that flow smoothly requires the combined input of the entire staff. Only in this way can we ensure that all needs will be met.

Some things to keep in mind as we undertake this task:

• The support space must be acoustically separate from the children's program to minimize distractions, yet visually linked to the reception area to provide easy access to parents coming to and from the center.

• The space must include some area for staff to get away for a moment of solitude and peace. It must also provide room for them to store and prepare classroom materials, type letters, run off notices, eat lunch, or just sit and relax.

• The support space must be situated so that administrative functions of the center can be conducted efficiently, but also acoustically buffered so that it does not interfere with conversations and conferences that might be going on.

• Finally, because this space is shared by so many individuals whose time is scarce, it is essential that the support space be easy to maintain. Work surfaces, cabinets, cupboards and the organization of equipment and supplies must be well delineated, clearly labeled, and constructed of materials that will endure considerable use.

Coping with clutter

"Order is Heaven's first law."

The sage that inspired the above inscription on the ceiling of the Library of Congress may have overstated the case for neatness. But most of us would agree that clutter does breed confusion and disorderliness interferes with straight thinking. Disorganization takes time and energy and keeps us from achieving our goals. But organization is not a moral issue, despite what our parents might have told us. There is no one correct way to organize, no one right order for everyone. Order is what works for the individual. And for each person that takes on different characteristics.

There are certain principles, however, that can help in our attempt to organize the support space in our early childhood environments. Organizing this space does not mean becoming rigid and inflexible. It means learning to see the whole picture and developing sensible patterns of behavior that encourage order. Like time management, organizing space does take more time at first, but far less of our time once our systems are in place and our organizing patterns become habit.

The wonderful thing about improving organizational skills is its impact on our morale and on the other people in our lives. As such, it may well be one of the more powerful antidotes for stress and burnout. So if you are coping with organization problems, or if you are a self-confessed clutterbug who says daily, "Boy, this place is a mess," and has to move a pile of things every time you want to sit down, you will find relief by applying a few of the tips in this section.

Don't allow things to accumulate that no longer have a real function: Ask yourself regularly, "Why do I need this item? Have I used it in the past week, month, year, decade?" Much of what we hold on to is junk, but our emotional attachments to it prevent us from giving or throwing it away. Five years' worth of educational supplies catalogs, puzzles with missing pieces, and class notes from our college days probably serve us little today. More often than not if we did need one of these old items we wouldn't know where to find it anyway. Assessing and reassessing the usefulness of items must go on constantly in a well-organized child care center. Schools tend to become repositories for other people's junk, anyway, and if we allow "things" to accumulate needlessly, it can squeeze us out of our space very quickly. The solution: Invest in several large waste baskets and use them daily. And get to know the recycling centers in your community where you can donate broken equipment and materials to be overhauled and given to needy children (or other needy schools).

Be selective about utilizing your storage space: Clutter tends to expand and to fill the space available. If you are a disorganized person with a small desk, your small desk will be cluttered. If you are a disorganized person with a large desk, your large desk will be cluttered. Being selective about saving something now that you could collect quickly when you need it will effectively increase your storage areas and reduce over-all frustration in locating items. For example, if you decided to do an art project using egg cartons, you could probably collect several dozen within a day or so if you just put up an "Egg Cartons Wanted" poster in the front of your school. Why use that scarce storage space now for 5000 egg cartons when keeping perhaps only half a dozen on hand for spontaneous projects would suffice? Other things we can generally get donated to us quickly include milk cartons, baby food jars, assorted cans, and cardboard tubes. Save your storage space for items more difficult to locate quickly like buttons, ribbons, greeting cards, feathers, pine cones, and miscellaneous gems and jewels for collage projects.

Compartmentalize when possible and store like items or items used together in close proximity to one another: The tape cassette player and extra tapes should be stored together. The same thing holds true for records and the record player, the broom and the dust pan, etc., etc. Following this principle not only saves steps but it makes locating something far easier. Items color-coded to specific storage areas decrease the possibility of losing or misplacing them. Keeping items in consistent locations is the key to effective use of space. If individuals who share space can predict where to find something, they can carry out their tasks with far less hassle. They will also be encouraged to return the item to the same location because they know others will be counting on finding it there when they need it. Assign a new space for each item bought and be sure potential users know where it is stored.

Clear your work surface of all unnecessary items before delving into a task: Not only does a cluttered desk or table top make an activity more difficult, but it is likely that something in one of those piles on the desk will distract your attention. We put things in stacks on our desk because we don't want to forget them. As we start to work on one project, our gaze wanders and catches something in one of those piles. Our concentration is interrupted and time is lost. Doing one important thing at a time is all we can ask of ourselves. Building organization in our work space to cut down on distractions helps us achieve better concentration and improves work habits.

Think of accessiblity and reflect the temporal in the way you organize items: When arranging equipment, supplies, reference books, and items used regularly make sure these things are convenient to reach and easy to return to their location. Items used less frequently can be stored on somewhat less accessible shelves. And items used only occasionally, like holiday decorations, can be stored in the least accessible areas of the center.

> **Tip:** Color-coded supplies trays for frequently used supplies like pencils, scissors, and staplers that often get "borrowed" from one location of the school and left elsewhere in the center can really help keep these essentials from disappearing. To make a supplies tray take a piece of plywood about 6" × 18". Attach to it four small tuna fish cans and two soup cans with Elmer's glue. Spray paint the entire board a bright color, using a different color for each tray. Put a small piece of colored

plastic tape that matches the board color on the stapler, scissors and tape dispenser. The outline of these items can be traced on the board to indicate where they belong. The containers can be used for paper clips, pencils, rubber bands, tacks, extra staples, etc. Place these boards in strategic places around the center. It will be then readily apparent when an item is not in its proper tray.

Invest in good equipment: Allocating money for equipment and materials involves difficult decisions when dollars are scarce. But machines that break down frequently or flimsy materials often end up costing more than had quality materials and equipment been bought in the first place. Too, we must add in time lost to repair machines as well as psychic stress and frustration. Quality costs more initially, but pays off in worker satisfaction and high morale.

Target one area to work on at a time: It is too easy to get discouraged at the enormity of the task if you feel that everything must be organized at once. Select just one drawer to begin with, then move selectively through the area. But be methodical: don't begin working on another part of the room before completing the first. Once you are satisfied with the organization of equipment, supplies and materials, share your new system with potential users of the area so that they will have a clear idea of your expectations for maintaining order.

If you're having difficulty getting started, sit down and determine the purpose you want to achieve in your organization of a specific area of the support space. Solutions to space problems should flow from our needs. For example, if you want to cut down on disruptions from machines and equipment, you might group these items together in a partitioned area of the adult work space. Or if you want to increase the teachers' use of a particular piece of equipment, you might locate it in a more accessible area.

Coordinating resource materials

Teacher effectiveness often turns on our ability to find that perfect book, poem, poster or artifact at the right moment to spark enthusiasm among our students. When Jeremy is bubbling over with excitement to show us the Monarch butterfly he captured earlier, it does us little good to lament that "Somewhere I have a poster that would be absolutely perfect . . . now where did I put it?" Chances are we've tucked it away somewhere between the purchase order for new carpentry equipment and last year's Halloween decorations.

But coordinating the multitude of resource materials that crosses the path of a teacher during the school term is a prodigious task. As with all our organizing principles, however, we have found that the system that works best is one specifically designed for our own program needs. Only in this way can we take into consideration our special spatial constraints, budget limitations, and the number of people who will be sharing the resource materials.

The following system has worked well for one child care center and is a good format from which you can adopt your own methods.

Children's books: When Jeremy brought in that butterfly, it would have been wonderful to be able to reach directly for Eric Carle's *Very Hungry Caterpillar Book* or a number of other children's books and resources that would have provided a springboard for discussion about caterpillars, cocoons, butterflies, and insects in general. The well-organized children's library will allow a teacher that kind of flexibility.

The first thing to do in organizing children's books is to look at the books you already have and determine what general categories they fall into. Now project what kinds of books you hope to add to your library and add categories for those as well. These categories will be tied to topical boxes and picture file organization later on.

Separate all your children's books into your chosen categories and designate a color of plastic tape (available at most variety or hardware stores) to go with each. Put a small strip of this tape on the lower edge of the binding of each book and store them on a bookcase in the teacher's prep area. Rotate out a dozen or so of these books each day to the classroom library area. The books will last longer and the children will appreciate them more.

Make a key for your book categories and post it next to the bookcase housing all the books in the staff room. For each new book added to the shelf, make a 3"×5" card indicating title, author and subject category. File it in a small box alphabetically by title next to the book shelf. In this way any parent participant, visiting student teacher, or classroom aide can immediately find the title of a particular book they are looking for.

Possible categories for your children's library:

- around the world, different cultures
- waterlife
- birds
- insects
- reptiles
- flowers, plantlife
- health and safety
- holidays
- feelings
- counting books
- animals (pets, zoo, farm, and wild)
- science discovery
- transportation
- dinosaurs, prehistoric man
- astronomy, the sun, moon, stars
- people, family, friends and community
- alphabet or word books
- body awareness, birth, death
- the four seasons
- colors
- miscellaneous story books

Tip: Construct a mini wall easel long enough to hold eight to ten books. Books can then be displayed face up on this easel—a good solution for organizing a children's book corner for easy access.

Picture files: Once we have developed the categories for our children's books, tying in appropriate pictures and posters that we have collected becomes easy. The most desirable method for storing pictures is to construct pull-out storage shelves approximately 20″ × 30″. Many programs do not have the space for such an elaborate setup. Alternatively, invest in large folders or envelopes (minimum size 18″×24″) and label boldly on the front of each the category of pictures and posters collected within. Art framing stores will often give away extra pieces of mat board to mount your favorite pictures. Otherwise favorites can be laminated or covered with clear contact paper to preserve them from fingerprints. To make your system work, however, the categories must correspond to the ones used for children's books. On the back of each new poster or picture, write the category that it will be stored under. This will make it easy for others borrowing your picture files to return loose pictures to their appropriate file.

> **Tip:** If your posters get mangled from improper storage, invest in a dozen or so mailing tubes and store the posters inside the tubes. Be sure to label the outside of the tube.

Topical boxes for curriculum aids: Organizing classroom curriculum materials that are too bulky for picture file folders is a headache. What generally happens is we stack that seashell or bird's nest in our supply closet somewhere and forget it. Why not collect a couple of dozen boxes all the same size? Cover with plain contact paper or paint with enamel-base paint. Put a bold label depicting the appropriate category of materials stored in each box so it can be plainly seen on the front of the box. These curriculum artifacts will only be used if they are accessible, so locate them in the teacher's prep area where things may be added as needed. Again, label each item that goes into the box if possible so that it can be returned to its correct category. These should correspond to the categories you have chosen for children's books and picture files. If you are really short on space, you may want to put two categories in one box.

Activity file boxes: Many new teachers feel overwhelmed at the thought of organizing the wealth of ideas they collect for classroom projects. One helpful method is to use the activity file box as the central organizing tool for assembling curriculum ideas.

As you read teacher magazines, clip out ideas that interest you. For the time being, just pile these in a file folder or box labeled "Treasure Chest of Ideas." Then designate one or two weeks during the year to do your major organizing.

Assemble about four 4" × 6" file boxes, several dividers for the boxes, and dozens of blank file cards that fit into the boxes. Jot down, type, or tape each idea collected from your miscellaneous slips onto the cards, *one activity per card.* Determine what category of the curriculum the activity is best suited for. Designate this heading on the top of the card along with the name of the activity, poem, or project. In the upper right hand corner code each card within the designated categories with a number. Each new card added gets the next number in that category. This will be used later on when we cross-reference these ideas to use in a curriculum theme.

The categories should be tailored to your own needs. Some possibilities include:

- art
- music/movement
- poetry/fingerplays
- reading readiness
- math readiness
- cooking/nutrition projects
- holidays
- seasons
- dramatic play
- science discovery

Records: The cost of individual albums makes it imperative that we devise a system for storing records that insures that they will be kept and maintained to last for many years. Find a box large enough to store albums upright facing forward. Separate and group the records within this box according to the type of music or activity on the record. Some possibilities:

- restful music for naptime
- classical background music
- jazz
- marching bands, rhythm activities
- counting songs and action games
- sing-along music

On the front of the box or in a separate file box, note what albums are grouped in each category. Each time you add a new album to your collection, label it with the category designation and insert in the appropriate grouping.

Field trip directory: Many schools waste valuable teacher time duplicating field trip information each time a group of children takes an excursion away from the center. Why not compile one directory that will serve the function of detailing all possible field trips within the community? This directory can then be updated each time a group goes on a specific field trip so all the information pertinent to the trip is current.

Some things to include on each page of your field trip guide:

- field trip location and directions on how to get there
- sample maps for parent or teachers driving the children
- dates that the field trip has been taken and the teacher's name
- suggested number of children
- contact person and telephone number
- appropriate dress
- admission charges, hours of operation
- travel time
- comments about the field trip and suggestions for future visits
- follow-up activity suggestions
- sample guides and literature from the field trip

Professional books—adults: There are many systems for organizing books for parents and staff. The one that will be most useful for you will revolve around the titles you have presently collected and those that you plan to add to your library in the future.

Teachers should have access to books of curriculum ideas or resource books for topics studied in the classroom. All other books can be housed in the parents' corner for parents to borrow.

Some possibilities for categories: You can use a tape method similar to the children's library book storage to insure that books are returned to the proper shelf. If you have put the colored tape around the lower edge of the binding on the children's books, tape the top edge of the binding for the adult books.

In the staff room	*In the parents' corner*
General education books	General parenting books
Curriculum books:	Child development books
art	Books on topics such as:
music/movement/drama	children's television
poetry/fingerplays	sibling rivalry
reading readiness	adoption
math readiness	fathering
science discovery	sex role identification
cooking/nutrition	birth/death
holidays/seasons	children's play
cultural awareness	general nutrition
health/safety	medical and health tips
	children's advocacy

Tip: Are your books frequently borrowed but never returned? Stamp the edges with your personal stamp or your school's name. This will be a visible reminder to your friends who have borrowed your volumes.

Cross reference binder: Assume that we want to do a unit or develop a theme in our classroom on the five senses. The cross reference binder helps us centralize our ideas from the resources we have in the classroom, so that we can duplicate the unit in the future while leaving the different parts intact to be utilized for other units. In the cross reference binder are a series of sheets that designate the resources collected to develop each theme. This binder can become the foundation for adding ideas to each time the theme is repeated.

You will want to develop your own format for each theme page but some of the things that should be included are detailed below.

Theme _____ Teacher _____

Goals of this unit_____

_____

_____

_____

_____

Resources to tap:

Children's books: _____

_____

Adult reference books: _____

_____

Songs/records: _____

_____

Poems/fingerplays: _____

_____

Art activity ideas: _____

_____

Science ideas: _____

_____

Math ideas: _____

_____

Science discovery: _____

_____

Field trip possibilities:_____

_____

Outside resources to contact: _____

_____

Films: _____

_____

Bulletin board and display ideas: _____

_____

Notes/comments: _____

_____

_____

_____

_____

_____

Tip: Forget what that prize bulletin board looked like? Capture your successes in photographs. Keep a camera handy to photograph those award-winning displays on bulletin boards and walls. Next time you want to duplicate the arrangement, it will be much easier with a photograph to remind you.

Buried under a paper avalanche?

The amount of paperwork involved in running a child care program is mind-boggling at times. The morass of forms, letters, memos, proposals, documents and reports that has proliferated to satisfy governmental, funding, and licensing agencies makes the organization of the administrative functions within the early childhood center difficult. Programs must also contend with cancelled checks, bank statements, receipts, correspondence, inventory records, purchase orders, minutes of meetings, and a variety of bookkeeping journals and accounting records that are part of running any small business.

Dealing with the paperwork jungle is not only time-consuming and expensive but many times downright frustrating. Administrative paperwork is one of the greatest sources of tension and stress for child care administrators. It is for this reason that it is particularly important that we focus attention on developing ways to handle paper efficiently and expeditiously.

Think thin—go on a paper diet! There are many things we can do daily to cut down on the time we spend handling paper. Most important is developing the in-today, out-tomorrow habit. The longer paper sits around, shuffled from pile to pile, the more time it eats up and the greater the likelihood that it will be misplaced or dates and deadlines missed altogether. Taking some kind of action each time a paper is handled is the first step to dealing effectively with the paper monster.

We are more likely to follow this practice if we create ways to expedite the movement of paper. Using the telephone instead of writing a reply is perhaps the quickest way to eliminate paper, but some situations don't lend themselves to this solution. When telephoning isn't possible, handwritten responses in the margin of letters or forms to be returned can cut down on typing time. Using postcards for quick notes, acknowledgements, and confirmations of appointments also cuts down on labor and saves postage as well.

Using form letters and window envelopes can help considerably in cutting down the volume of paper and the time it takes to handle correspondence. When designing a new form, think about what you want to accomplish. Ask yourself what steps might be simplified, what forms might be consolidated, and what procedures might be eliminated without hampering the efficiency of your operation.

When developing a new form, make sure that all instructions are printed right on the form itself, and that sufficient space is available for checklist, written responses, or office notations once the form has been turned in. It is also helpful to include a title and number on each form as well as the date that the form was written or revised.

Try to keep forms the same size but vary the color of paper each year to aid in sorting and updating information. And destroy old forms. Don't even allow them to be used for recycled paper in your classroom. Many a parent has been confused when an art masterpiece has come home on the back of an announcement the relevance of which they are not quite sure.

Tip: An idea for revisions: During the course of the year we often get thoughts on how we would like to revise a form we use regularly. Why not keep a notebook that

has one copy of each form used in the school? Jot your
revision notations on this sample. Then when it is time
to do a complete revision of the form, all your thoughts
will be collected and ready to organize in a new format.

Many times we may feel that a form is too impersonal for the
information we want to convey. But still much of our general correspondence is similar in nature. Why not develop a system for
composing letters from guide paragraphs? Guide paragraphs are
usually better written because we have taken the time to compose
them carefully. This method also saves time in dictating, because
the guide paragraphs can be referred to by number for the typist.

A handy guide for setting up a letter file of forms and guide
letters is available from the Superintendent of Documents.
Request:

"Managing Correspondence: Form and Guide Letters"
   Stock #2203–00903
U.S. Government Printing Office
Washington, D.C. 20402

Avoiding paper pollution: Developing the fine art of
wastebasketry is perhaps the most important organizing skill we
can cultivate to prevent being inundated by needless paper. Keeping the wastebasket handy as you sort through the daily mail helps
dispose of needless mail immediately.

Tip: If you feel that you are receiving more than your
fair share of junk mail these days, there are steps that
you can take to reduce the number of pieces you
receive. Write to the Mail Preference Service and ask
that your name be eliminated from the wholesale mailing
list in their control. Their address is:

Mail Preference Service
Direct Mail Marketing
6 East 43rd Street
New York, N.Y. 10017

Good paper control begins with selective sorting and screening. A good system is one that works for you; but most effective

paper managers find that developing a sorting method for information helps reduce unnecessary shuffling of paper. As you open the mail each day, weed out the trivia and file in the circular file. Information from memos announcing the important meetings, giving directions, or supplying dates and facts on upcoming events can be immediately transferred to your calendar and plan book. Then these miscellaneous pieces of paper can be thrown away.

For all the items remaining, assign temporary "parking places" such as these:

- *Panic file:* These are items that must get done *today*. Nothing goes into this pile that you do not intend to work on today. At the end of the day this tray should be empty except for a few items that may need your attention on the following day.

- *Pending:* In this pile are a series of colorful files labeled to identify projects or activities awaiting some action. You might find it helpful to tack a small slip of paper on the front of each file to include information such as due date for project completion, names and telephone numbers of contact people, and addresses for sending correspondence that relates to the activity. This slip should also include space to indicate action being taken to appraise others who share the material how the project is progressing. This cuts down on time spent in refamiliarizing ourselves with the contents of the file each time we open it.

- *Financial:* Except in very large early childhood centers, bills and financial statements can be collected for attention on two dates during the month (like the 1st and the 20th) when all financial matters can be attended to at once.

- *Five-minute tasks:* These might include the postcard responses, marginal notes on letters, short lists to be compiled and other quick tasks that need attention. These items can be put in your plan book, tote bag, or brief case and taken with you to do when you might have a few extra minutes between other activities.

- *Reading material:* Put all journals, magazines, newsletters from organizations, and other items to read in a big basket to take home. Block out a couple of evenings during the month to plow through them, skimming information and clipping articles that should be saved and read in depth later on.

Developing a comprehensive filing system

Retrieval is the name of the game for filing. If we don't know we have something or can't find it when we need it, what we have filed has little value. Most school administrators would agree that 80 percent or more of what we tuck away in four file cabinets never gets referred to again, not even once. Most of what we store away has little consequence to the success of our center. We cling to the notion that we may need this or that piece of paper "some day," so we accumulate files and records year after year, never bothering to thin them out.

The best filing systems are simple and tailored to specific program needs. A good filing system is not static. Each time a file is used we should sort through, refresh our memory of its contents, and dispose of outdated information and material. Such a method also insures that our files change as the program changes and adapts to our needs. Most effective filing systems keep fewer files rather than too many, and keep files general rather than too specific. It is easier to go through one file with twenty papers than through ten files with two papers each.

When setting up a filing system initially, decide how new information will be added. Will it be inserted in the front or rear of the folder? Whatever method is adopted should be employed consistently. Fast retrieval also comes from knowing how and where to file papers initially. Instead of asking ourselves, "Where can I put this piece of paper?" we should ask, "What will I be thinking of when I will want this paper again?" When we have decided on the appropriate file, we should then write that heading in the top corner of each paper to be filed. This takes an extra moment initially but insures that our files will be maintained consistently by others adding to or returning information to our file folders.

Tip: Keep your file cabinet close to your telephone. That way, when someone puts you on hold, you can get some miscellaneous filing done.

Where do we begin in establishing a comprehensive filing system? First, think of the broad categories applicable to your program. Then refine those categories by including files headings

specific to your individual program needs. Leave extra space in the file drawer to allow for reasonable expansion of the categories. Overstuffed drawers cause needless frustration. Once you have established the broad categories and specific file headings within each of those categories, type up this information on a small card and post it on the front of each file drawer. Then as you revise the files in each drawer make the appropriate notation on the card. Only in this way will you be continually current on your changing needs.

The following delineation of files is an example of one method used in an early childhood center.

Editor's note: Readers wishing to order a packet of sample forms and handbooks developed by Paula Jorde-Bloom may write directly to her c/o New Horizons, P.O. Box 863, Lake Forest, Illinois 60045. (Items included are followed by an *)

File It!

School Administration

- Articles of Incorporation
- Bylaws
- Board of Directors—general
- Board of Directors—minutes of meetings

Finance and Fund Raising

- Budget—current
- Budget—previous years
- Fund raising events—general
- Fund raising activities (specifically labeled)
- Grant proposals—previous years
- Purchase order form
- Scholarship application form*
- Tax exempt status information
- Quarterly withholding statements—current year
- Quarterly withholding statements—previous 3 years
- Federal and State Tax returns—previous 3 years

Insurance

- State disability insurance
- Unemployment compensation insurance
- Liability insurance
- Automobile insurance
- Health insurance

Enrollment

- General letter to parents requesting information*
- Application form*
- School brochure*
- Acceptance letter*
- Current tuition schedule*
- Tuition agreement form
- School calendar
- Health & Immunization record*

- Emergency form*
- Carpool letter*
- Re-enrollment form*
- School roster
- Waiting list letter*

Space and Equipment

- Office equipment warranties
- Office supplies inventory form
- Office equipment catalogs
- Office equipment maintenance record
- Educational equipment warranties (includes playground)
- Educational supplies inventory form
- Educational equipment catalogs
- Educational equipment maintenance record
- Janitorial service checklist*
- Keys check-out record

Health & Safety

- School accident report form*
- Communicable diseases chart*
- First-aid procedures checklist*
- Fire drill procedures checklist
- Earthquake/natural disaster checklist
- Health and safety handouts for parents

Nutrition

- Child Care Food Program menus
- Food Program reimbursement forms
- Guidelines for nutritious snacks*
- Nutrition handouts for parents

Parent Relations

- Parents' handbook*
- Newsletter ideas
- Past newsletters*

- Parenting books bibliography*
- Parent resource questionnaire*
- Letter to departing parents*
- Program evaluation form for parents*
- Parent participant guidelines*
- Parent orientation
- Classroom observation guidelines*
- Selected parenting handouts

Staffing

- Employment application*
- Job announcements
- Job descriptions
- Letter to applicants not hired*
- Contract form*
- W-4 withholding form
- Staff policy handbook
- Emergency form for staff*
- Record of staff absences
- Staff evaluation form*
- Teacher in-service ideas
- Volunteers and substitutes
- Staff roster
- Individual employee files:
  - W-4
  - W-2's from previous years
  - application/resume/transcripts
  - letters of reference
  - sick leave record
  - evaluations
  - current contract
  - TB clearance

- physician's statement of good health
- driver's license number and emergency information
- notes on current performance

Community Relations

- Consultant services available
- Referral agencies
- Articles and press releases about program
- Child advocacy issues
- Sample brochures, descriptive literature from community counseling, health, and family service agencies
- Professional organizations
- Classified advertising rates and samples

Children

- Skills inventory form*
- Conference request form*
- Conference follow-up form
- Individual child's file
  - emergency information
  - application and supporting materials
  - progress notes
  - health and immunization record
  - skills inventory and evaluations
  - conference follow-up notes
  - selected samples of work

Program

- Classroom curriculum guidelines
- Fieldtrip notification form*
- Group assignments
- Classroom procedures and guidelines*

- Special events: puppeteers, visiting zoo, clowns, magicians
- Classroom schedules
- Rotating responsibilities
- Bright ideas for curriculum activities

Chapter 5
Managing People

The Essence of Leadership

*"You do not lead by hitting people over the head . . .
That's assault, not leadership."*

Dwight Eisenhower

Child care centers are more than physical structures performing specific functions. They are also complex social systems with intricate networks of interpersonal relationships. As in other human service organizations, success in a child care center depends on the quality of personal interactions. If the center is healthy, it is constantly growing, adapting to change and effectively utilizing its most valuable resource—its people. Such an environment conveys to staff, parents, children, and community a feeling of warmth and genuine concern. But achieving this kind of organizational climate does not occur by happenstance. It is the product of carefully exercised leadership.

Traditionally, it is the director of the center who sets the emotional climate of the organization. As its most visible leader, the director must balance short-term needs with long-term goals and create an environment based on mutual respect in which individuals may grow and be nourished. But leadership is not the exclusive domain of the center director. Teachers, in their daily work with parents, classroom aides, student teachers and volunteers, must also make leadership decisions by organizing and guiding individuals toward achieving program goals.

In this section we shall explore some of the characteristics at the heart of good leadership in the early childhood setting. We will look at ways that directors and teachers motivate, build co-operation, and establish a base of mutual trust with individuals. We will also examine how good leaders are able to maintain a balance between organizational needs and personal needs and keep themselves growing, reaching, in control, and immune to the effects of the burnout syndrome.

There is no easy formula for learning effective leadership skills. The principles of good management must be personalized to fit the individual's style and unique set of circumstances. But they can be studied, practiced, and refined. As program administrators and teachers we can learn to apply effective techniques for guiding the mental and physical energies of the people with whom we work. In the process, we can achieve that all-important balance of meeting our own needs as well.

Exercise 31
How effective am I in my leadership role?

	yes	no

1. Do I do the work of several people and do many things that are not in line with my job description? ⎯ ⎯

2. Do I always seem swamped with yesterday's crises, always fighting fires, meeting deadlines, and living on the edge of disaster? ⎯ ⎯

3. Am I burdened with more paperwork than I was a year ago? ⎯ ⎯

4. Do I find people waiting for my approval or opinion for tasks that they should be assuming on their own? ⎯ ⎯

5. Do I receive a lot of work-related telephone calls at home in the evening and on weekends? ⎯ ⎯

6. Do I dread leaving the center for a long weekend or a short vacation because of the mountain of work that will accumulate in my absence? ⎯ ⎯

7. Do I spend more time working on details than on planning and supervising activities with my staff? ⎯ ⎯

8. Do I find that I have to repeat directions, suggestions, and comments over and over before they are followed through? ⎯ ⎯

9. Do I feel that I have to remind my staff in subtle ways how hard I work because I don't think they understand and appreciate how much I do? ⎯ ⎯

10. Does my work consume my whole life, rarely allowing time to pursue other outside interests and activities? ⎯ ⎯

Can I survive without an organizational chart?

"To lead people is to walk behind them."

Lao-tzu

The traditional hierarchy of an organization is usually seen as a pyramid. The leader on the top disseminates information downward and controls the direction of the operation. But the challenge of good leadership, be it as center director or as a classroom teacher, is to see if we can manage, direct, and motivate others as though we had no rank and had to depend on the quality of our ideas as exemplified through our daily example.[1]

In some ways, the traditional organizational chart demotivates people. Most of us do not like to think of ourselves as below someone else.[2] If we really want a model to reflect role responsibilities, an inverse pyramid might be more appropriate. Here the leader at the tiny base perceives the role as one of supporting those above, so that they can carry out the goals of the school.

It is true that with some titles we inherit a certain amount of authority. But the fine art of leading is to use that authority wisely and sparingly. Contrary to some popular theories, power and loyalty are not achieved by controlling people. Authority derived from manipulating others through rewards and punishments is a poor substitute for leadership. Leadership is not a question of clever maneuvering to use position to garner respect. On the contrary, respect comes from helping individuals discover their own inner aspirations, motives, and needs, and helping them work collectively to accomplish group goals. The best organizations take on the dynamics of people working around a circle, supporting, helping, and guiding one another.[3]

In this guiding and supporting role we are mindful that good leadership equals good modeling. The truism that our actions speak louder than our words is at the core of motivational theory. All the nonverbal things we do conveys far more than our verbal exhortations. Individuals who have a caring, open, expressive, and enthusiastic style that is consistent with their goals usually find that these traits filter down through their programs.

Providing the emotional sustenance that helps individuals to stretch and grow is the cornerstone of good leadership. But our ability to draw others to us and nourish them is directly related to our own base of security and how we perceive that our own needs are being met.[4] Our level of defensive behavior on the job correlates with our personal satisfaction. If we feel fulfilled, we are in a better position to help and guide others. On the other hand, if we feel unsure of ourselves, threatened, overworked, or taken advantage of, our interactions with others will clearly convey these insecurities.

But personal needs and organizational needs are not mutually exclusive. Reconciling the needs of others with our own is complicated precisely because the two domains are intricately tied together. Our level of fulfillment rests in large part on how well we are achieving our organizational objectives. It is a circular process in many ways. Our actions in motivating, guiding, and helping others allows them to work to achieve program goals. And achieving a smooth-flowing organization in turn makes us feel needed and worthwhile. If the cycle is positive, it will generate positive feelings. If it is negative, it will generate negative undercurrents and overall dissatisfaction and insecurity.

Applying motivational theory to early childhood education

In assessing our own leadership style, we must take a close look at some of the assumptions we have about how individuals are best motivated in a school environment. The research of several eminent psychologists in motivational theory will provide the framework for this analysis.

The work of Douglas McGregor serves as a good starting point because it forces us to analyze our assumptions about the people who work for us.[5] McGregor postulates that there are essentially two ways that leaders view individuals in the work setting. Theory X holds that people dislike to work and that they will avoid it at all costs if they can. In this view individuals avoid challenge and responsibility, and most people look for security in a job. Applying this philosophy dictates that the leadership role is one of controlling, directing, coercing, and perhaps even threatening individuals to do what they should.

Theory Y, on the other hand, contends that work is natural for people. It states they need it and want it, and that work is an extension of their being. Individuals work toward things to which they are committed, and this commitment is the basis of job satisfaction. Under the right conditions, people will not only accept responsibility but seek it. Ascribing to this philosophy means that as a leader we put faith in our employees to challenge their own creative energy to meet those inner needs.

Teachers and directors in leadership roles who accept this premise of human motivation embrace the notion that individuals are their own best source of motivation.[6] If the work is properly structured, people will be motivated by the results of their labors more than by external rewards, punishment, or controls imposed by others.

The work of Abraham Maslow also brings to our awareness an understanding of the motivational needs of people.[7] Maslow postulates that we proceed up a hierarchy of needs, fulfilling basic needs first before striving and reaching for the next level. At the bottom of the hierarchy are the physiological-deficiency needs. Food, shelter, sleep, sex, security and freedom from threat are some of these lower-level needs. Once they are satisfied, the individual moves on to satisfying more internal needs that form the basis for self-fulfillment and self-expression.

The research conducted by Frederick Herzberg and by Henry Murray[8] further illustrates the conditions that create a climate for job satisfaction—that human beings are motivated by attending to internal needs once the basic external factors are met in a job environment. From these insights we can draw certain generalizations that apply to the early childhood environment.

To feel satisfied and productive in their roles as child care workers, individuals have three essential needs that must be addressed:

• The need for affiliation: to be with friends and colleagues who are caring, supportive, and appreciative.

• The need for achievement: To feel useful, challenged, and recognized for work well done.

- The need for involvement: To be able to make decisions about things which directly affect them.

An understanding of these motivational needs illuminates a direction of personal growth in the child care profession. It provides the basis for improving organizational structure reducing the incidence of stress and burnout.

Cultivating a Sense of Community: Meeting the Need for Affiliation

"A little kindness from person to person is better than a vast love for all of humankind."

We know from the research conducted on burnout that people engaged in mutually supportive relationships cope better with the stresses inherent in their personal and professional lives. By working with others who care and share, they gain an increased understanding of themselves, and develop more realistic coping strategies to deal with the stressors that confront them.

People who enter the child care field usually have a sense of mission. They are compassionate and caring. But the treadmill of activity that consumes their time and energy on the job often keeps them from establishing close relationships with others. Time pressures, the demanding nature of the role, and the physical layout of the child care environment are some of the barriers that prevent staff from exchanging information, sharing ideas and lending and receiving support with one another.

As administrators of child care programs, we must conciously strive to structure ways of cultivating closeness within our work environments. For a sense of community on the job not only provides the social support that nourishes the spirit, but provides the impetus that makes individuals strive for optimal performance as well. The staff, the children, and their families all benefit from such a situation.

Building a sense of community rests in large measure on our ability to develop a team spirit and shared goals, and our ability to implement these goals with effective delegating and communicating skills. The remainder of this section will focus on these areas of concern.

The concept of sharedness

Central to the director's role as leader is developing a team spirit among the staff. Much like the conductor of a symphony, the child care director knows that the combined energy of a group working in harmony creates a "whole" that is greater than the sum of its parts. The same model, of course, can be applied to the classroom setting where the teacher coordinates the activities of aides and volunteers by creating a unified team.

The concept of sharedness is an integral part of developing this team spirit.[9] Sharedness is the degree to which individuals are accepting of other points of view, and the degree to which they understand and value the needs of others. It means that the entire group works as a collective body and understands that achieving group goals transcends individual wishes.

But teamwork doesn't just happen. It is a difficult task, indeed, to weld divergent personalities and conflicting viewpoints and needs into a unified harmonious effort. Some suggest that women in particular have difficulty in this aspect of the management role because they have not been conditioned for team play.[10] Men have had a lifelong training to be flexible and cooperative and to work within a network to achieve goals. Even as young boys in playing sports, they learned the lessons of team effort. Vince Lombardi put it succinctly when he said, "If they succeed, the team succeeds, and if the team succeeds, they succeed!"[11] Women tend to want to be self-sufficient, to go it alone, to shoulder the burden themselves rather than investing energy to create a team spirit where all share responsibility (and the glory) of achievement.

That is not to say that all women have been conditioned to operate this way. Nor that once aware of this difference in upbringing, women can't take conscious steps to employ effective techniques to build and develop a sense of sharedness. As leaders they can stress group goals and make sure that each person knows what others in the group are trying to accomplish. They can tie individual success to group success, emphasizing each person's contributions to the group. They can promote cooperation and point out specifically how individuals can help one another. And they can convey to others that how well individuals work with one another is one of the measures of their performance.

Finally, team spirit is developed when channels are open for people to discuss and keep fully informed of the inner workings of the center. One informal way to cultivate a sense of community and team spirit is the daily "focus time." Different centers employ a variation of this and call it different names, but the concept and the purpose are essentially the same. The staff congregates for five to ten minutes before the program begins each day and quickly exchanges information of interest to the entire group. This does not take the place of regular staff meetings which are devoted to problem-solving or group-decision-making.

Focus time is merely a very quick opportunity for individual staff to apprise others of special projects that are going to take place that day, field trips that are scheduled, any mini-crises that have developed in the last 24 hours, and any unusual events that affect the entire group (like illness among staff or students). If adhered to regularly, this session will become the backbone of good communication in the center. It will also save time in the long run by eliminating overlapping responsibilities, fuzzy authority, and unclear procedures. It is imperative, however, that this daily focus time not exceed ten minutes if it is going to serve its purpose and not develop into an added burden for workers.

The fine art of delegating

Why are some leaders more enjoyable to work for than others? When much of running an early childhood program is routine, how is it that some individuals are able to get and keep people enthusiastic, hardworking, and dedicated? The answer in large part rests in their ability to delegate effectively.

Getting work done through others is central to the leadership role. Good leaders have refined the art of delegating by challenging people with assignments that match their mental and physical capabilities. They stretch people and help them develop ways to do their jobs more creatively and more interestingly. The benefits of good delegation are multifold: it provides job enrichment for the staff; it makes them a more integral part of the operation; it builds a more unified team spirit; and it forces us to be more organized. More than anything else, though, delegating means multiplying ourselves and increasing our ability to accomplish more in less time.

Delegating makes the leader the facilitator instead of the doer of everything. At the same time, it provides opportunities for others to demonstrate their abilities beyond the day-to-day routine tasks. The bonus from the director's viewpoint is that when functions are delegated, teachers also gain a greater appreciation and insight into the dimensions of the administrative role. If we are serious about reducing stress and the pressures that are part of the job of directing a center, we must give priority to perfecting our ability to delegate.

If delegating is so advantageous to our own mental health and the effective operation of our program, why do we so often resist employing these skills? How often do we say to ourselves:

- "No one can do the job as well as I can."
- "No one can do it as fast as I can."
- "When I do it I know it'll get it done right."
- "I don't want to burden anyone else with more work."
- "No one has enough interest (background or knowledge) to do the task."

We've built up a whole panoply of convenient, tried-and-true excuses for not delegating. But if we examine our own motives, we may discover the illogic in our rationalizations.

One reason we are reluctant to delegate is that we consciously or unconsciously resist letting go. But delegating does not mean abdicating responsibility. Moreover, holding on to too many tasks and responsibilities implies a lack of trust in others to perform particular tasks competently. This decreases motivation in the long run.

In the end we find that most of our excuses are short-term justifications. It is true, there is always an element of risk in turning over an assignment to someone else. And delegating does take more time initially—time spent in planning, communicating the scope of the task, supervising the activity and giving feedback. But we have to ask ourselves: Are we willing to go on playing the martyr, trying to do too much, assuming too much responsibility, and shouldering too many burdens single-handedly?

But learning to delegate with tact and finesse can be difficult. Delegating does not mean dumping unpleasant tasks on people. It means assessing with individuals those areas in which they would like to assume more responsibility and then structuring work assignments to fit.

In our assessment of our job responsibilities, we have to isolate the tasks that only we can do. Then we have to scrutinize the remaining aspects of our role and ask the following questions:

• Is there anyone who can do this particular activity better or with less expense than I can?

• Is there anyone who can do this task as well as I can even though it may take a bit longer at first?

• Is there anyone who would enjoy doing this task more than I do?

We can't assume that just because one aspect of our job is unpleasant for us that it will be for another person. One classroom teacher found, for instance, that she tended to procrastinate writing the monthly newsletter until the very last minute. When she suggested "relinquishing" the responsibility of writing the newsletter to her aide, much to her surprise the aide eagerly volunteered even though it meant much of the work had to be done in the evenings at first. Eventually job assignments were adjusted to incorporate this activity into the aide's regular work hours.

The following ten steps to effective delegation may be helpful as you develop and refine your delegating skills.

1. *Before delegating a task or activity, crystallize in your own mind exactly what you want to accomplish.* In other words, if the task were to be done perfectly, what would the results look like? By delegating for those specific results as clearly as possible, it becomes much easier to structure the activity and formulate realistic standards of performance.

2. *Select the right person for the right task.* Who on your staff has the time, interest, expertise, and motivation to take on the job? Success in large part will be determined by the appropriate match of people to activities. The better we know our staff, the better we will be able to assess and work with them to determine the right fit.

3. *Organize, collect information, and formulate the scope of the assignment before delegating.* It is far better to have all the materials and information the person will need to get started than dribbling out bits and pieces of the assignment over a period of time. In this way the person doing the task will have a clearer picture of its scope at the outset.

4. *The manner in which a task is delegated may determine how it is received and the spirit in which the person carries out the activity.* Our tone of voice, our thoroughness, and the respect we convey in delegating sets the climate for accepting the responsibility. The individual must feel that the task makes a worthwhile contribution to the overall program. Let the person know, also, how the task frees up your time to pursue other activities that help the center. This is particularly important when dealing with volunteers in the classroom. Because they are not receiving financial remuneration, the psychic wage volunteers receive for their hard work is even more important. They need to know that their contribution of time and energy is appreciated and valued.

5. *Insure that the ways of measuring performance are mutually understood.* Does the person know the task's deadline? Are the criteria of completion clearly understood? During the initial sharing, solicit as much feedback as possible to make sure you are both in agreement.

6. *Try to avoid overlapping responsibility.* When individuals work closely with one another overlapping functions may cause competition, tension, and job uncertainty. Make sure the person knows how the particular activity is different from others in the center.

7. *Follow up verbal delegation with written instructions.* A quick note summarizing expectations is particularly useful for activities that may span several weeks or months. This will help keep standards for performance clear and provide an avenue for the person to clarify any fuzzy areas of instruction.

8. *Help the individual work for visible results.* A sense of closure is important when we take on assignments. Try to delegate the whole activity from start to finish. There is a strong sense of satisfaction that goes from working on the total rather than contributing to a small part. When possible, assign tasks that allow the person to carry through the responsibility from conception to completion.

9. *Provide feedback and follow-up from a distance.* Once you delegate, get out of the person's way. Allow them room to make mistakes, work at their own pace, and handle their own problems. Provide checkpoints along the way where you can provide guidance and feedback, but monitor progress with a respect for the individual's need to be independent.

"A teacher we know of who liked to keep a watch on every small detail handed over a project to a classroom aide and immediately asked how long it would take. "About two hours," the aide said. "But if you stand over me, it may take two days!"

10. *Call in the experts:* Good delegating extends beyond our immediate staff. From janitorial help, gardening, and car maintenance to finding a consultant to conduct a survey for our center, there are dozens of ways that delegating can drastically cut down on our total commitments. In fact, a quick glance through

the Yellow Pages will convince us that there is a service available for just about any kind of task we can dream up. With friends (or the parents of our students), it may be possible to exchange services or barter our talents to do something that we can do quicker and enjoy more for a service that we dislike or is too difficult. Other services we may have to pay to have done. But in trying to decide whether or not to pick up the telephone and call for any particular service, we must work into the equation our cost in time and energy for not having something else do it. We may find that having experts do the job will be more efficient because it frees up valuable time for us to pursue higher priority items.

Effective communication—the mortar that holds the team together

"Wise men speak because they have something to say,
Fools speak because they have to say something"

Plato

Communication is an elusive concept that involves a circular process of sharing one's ideas and feelings with others and interpreting the feedback received.[12] In many ways, effective leadership in early childhood education is synonymous with effective communication because the success of a child care program relies so heavily on the open, honest exchange of information, ideas, and feelings. Good communication is the lubricating oil that makes all the parts of an operation run smoothly and effectively.

Many directors and teachers say they want a good rapport and know that open communication is essential to a healthy organization. But their actions and nonverbal messages often discourage openness and block people from openly expressing their opinions. If we believe in the merits of good communication and want to facilitate it in our individual programs, we must keep our ego out of the equation. We have to do away with the defensive messages from us that prevent people from being open. We must make our actions congruent with our spoken messages in conveying our sincerity.

The nature of the child care business guarantees that there will always be some misunderstandings and problems in human relationships. But what distinguishes good programs, where communication channels are open and direct, is that these misundstandings are infrequent. When they do occur, grievances and problems are dealt with quickly and vigorously.

Good communication skills can be learned and deliberately applied in the child care setting. The following techniques culled from a variety of resources will be helpful.

Ask yourself what you want to accomplish in an exchange with another person: If we have a clear image in our own minds of the result we want by the end of the conversation, often the steps and methods we should use will fall clearly in place. If we don't know precisely what we want to accomplish, we may communicate what we think we should say or what we think the other person wants to hear instead of what is needed to accomplish our purpose.

Avoid generalities when describing people or things: There is a real temptation to rely on vague words like good, bad, shy, aggressive, and hostile when talking to parents and staff about children in a school setting. Loaded words are easily open to misinterpretation. Try to give specific examples to illustrate what you want to say. If you can't think of a specific example, perhaps you don't really mean what you were going to say anyway.

Check your tone: It is not what we say but how we say it that usually determines how the other person interprets what we have said. What he/she "hears" may totally negate our verbal communication. We must be sensitive to the manner in which we convey a message to another person. Our tone is one of the strongest traits of our style of relating to other people. It must be consistent with our feelings and what we want to accomplish from a conversation.

Make your words and nonverbal actions congruent: Just as the tone of our voice plays an important role in the success we have in communicating our message, so too do the nonverbal nuances that are part of our communicating style. Our personal mannerisms in terms of dress, gestures, eye contact, sitting or standing position, and other expressive features carry powerful messages which can strengthen or weaken what we hope to communicate. Some communications researchers believe that fully 60 percent of all communication between people is based on body language. This is particularly true in the first few minutes of contact. Opinions derived from body signals form a strong basis of accepting or rejecting what the person is about to say. If we want words and body language to be consistent and reinforce what we want to convey, we must give careful consideration to this dimension of the communicating process.

Avoid indirect communication whenever possible: Since gestures, facial expressions, and body language in general are so important in communicating our message, it behooves us to try to avoid nonpersonal exchanges (like telephone conversations) when the content of what we are communicating may in the slightest way be misconstrued or open to misinterpretation. The better you know a person and the longer and more established your relationship, the safer it is to communicate in nondirect ways. With parents, board members, and community contacts, strive first for personal contact building trust and establishing rapport before relying predominantly on written communications or telephone conversations.

Try to visualize your ideas for other people: It is easier to grasp an abstraction if we can relate it to something concrete. People who communicate well are able to draw pictures with their words. They create images that express what they hope to convey in simple, precise ways that help people understand and remember what has been said to them.

Don't hesitate to ask for clarification: Many times when we don't understand what has been said to us, we hesitate to say so. Fuzzy, unclear communication is a barrier to good interpersonal relationships. We need to feel the confidence to say, "I'm not quite sure I understand you," or "What do you mean by that?" Asking people tactfully to rephrase and clarify what they say can have the added benefit of allowing the other person to do the same to you if what you have said is unclear.

Don't ask a question or give a choice when there isn't one: We learn quickly when dealing with young children that when we word a command like a question ("Johnny, don't you want to clean up now?") or tag on an "okay" ("Let's all put away the blocks, okay?"), children quickly pick up on our lack of decisiveness. The same rule applies to adults as well. Making a direct request to a staff person should be done so as to convey what we want done and by when with tact and firmness.

Be aware of how inanimate objects can effect communication: A desk, seating arrangement, a poorly positioned table, or other furniture can all be barriers to communication. To facilitate open communication with other people, we must pay attention to the way we utilize our physical space to reflect the messages we want to convey. Even the distance between chairs in a seating arrangement or the height differences between standing and sitting individuals can be barriers to an open exchange.

Try not to overcommunicate: Perhaps the hardest part of talking is knowing when to stop. Rambling, forgetting the point, repetition, and overdetailing not only confuses people (and bores them) but also takes up valuable time. Don't cloud the main point of what you want to say. Say it and stop talking.

Respect the importance of good timing: How an individual receives a request or handles a conversation has a lot to do with the appropriate time and place. People can be unnerved if we interrupt their concentration or disrupt an activity to ask a question, make a request, or begin a conversation. We need to respect their needs by asking them, "Is this a good time for us to talk about. . .?" By extending this respect, we are also conveying the message that we appreciate the same courtesy in return.

Be an active listener: Talking is only half the equation in good communication. Of equal importance is learning to be an empathetic, attentive listener. There is an old saying, "Since we were given only one mouth but two ears, perhaps we were meant to listen twice as much as we talk."[13] There's a great deal of truth in that remark that can help us improve our communicating skills. Active listening is difficult. Our minds tend to race ahead and think of what we are going to say next, or get sidetracked with wandering thoughts. Acknowledging responses, nodding, and reflecting back what the other person has said demonstrates that we are indeed interested and that we care and are concerned. Restating in our own words what the person has said also clears up any misunderstanding in what was communicated. Sensitive listening skills are rare, but if we are serious about opening communication channels, we must let others know that we are receptive to feedback. This does not mean that we have to agree with what is being expressed. It only means that we have to convey to others that we appreciate their openness and that they have given us a clearer understanding of the picture. Some phrases that might be helpful:

- "I understand how you feel now."
- "Thank you for being so open with me."
- "What would you like me to do?"
- "I am concerned about how you feel about. . ."

Sometimes written communication is best: Sometimes what we need to communicate can best be transmitted in a written memo. Written notes can also serve as useful follow-ups by highlighting the main points of a conversation noting deadlines and restating specific requests. In this way we are not relying on the person's memory to follow through. But just as we take pains to be precise, thoughtful, and direct verbally, we need to exercise the same skills in written communciation. It is imperative that we develop good habits of clear, concise communication. Clarity means shortness, simplicity, and precision in words. Covering too many topics and being too verbose overwhelms the reader. Given too much data to absorb or too many written communications, people are not able to distinguish the important from the trivial, and may end up rejecting or not reading it.

Before writing a memo, ask yourself what you hope to accomplish. Each sentence should bring you closer to that objective. The most important rule in written communication is to *keep it simple.* Don't try to dazzle people with your vocabulary or your technical know-how. Organize your thoughts in a logical fashion, and stick to your salient points without catch-all phrases that are vague and not easily understood. "Psychobabble" benefits no one.

The essence of good communication is to say what you need to say in as direct a way as possible. Remember, the Lord's Prayer has only 71 words, the Ten Commandments 297, and the Gettysburg Address only 268. Keep sentences and paragraphs short, keep to the point, and remember:

"It is not enough to write merely to be understood.
We must write so that we cannot possibly be misunderstood!"[14]

Staffing for Performance:
Meeting the Need for Achievement

Good leaders know that people are not machines. Machines can be worked, humans must be developed.[15] This distinction is critical to early childhood programs because of its implications for the way that directors spend time with teachers and staff. Because the success of child care programs depends so heavily on the performance of its people, staffing must be paramount in the role responsibilities of the program director. Keep in mind, however, that the classroom teacher involved in supervising student teachers and aides can also apply these same principles of training.

People cannot be hired, turned loose, and expected to perform at optimal levels. Good staffing means planning, training, and evaluating together to guarantee built-in opportunities for job enrichment and personal achievement. It is the leader's responsibility to create conditions conducive to optimal staff performance, allowing individuals to excel in their roles.

It may be useful to view this aspect of the leadership role as a *performance triangle* with planning, training, and evaluating each comprising corners of the scheme.

THE PERFORMANCE TRIANGLE

Planning

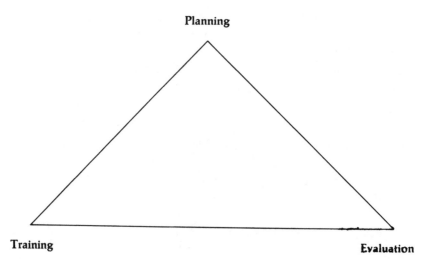

Training

Evaluation

Staffing for performance entails getting to know each staff person through a joint *planning* session that helps define the scope of the individual's role and responsibilities. The director is the only one to have a total overview of the operation and how each person fits into that picture, much like fitting together the pieces of a jigsaw puzzle. The planning sessions give each person on the staff a broader perspective of where they fit into the scheme and how their job relates with others.

Too often we look at job descriptions and try to mold the person into a particular role. But real stretching of human resources comes from looking at the individual first and defining the job around that person. Each time a new person is hired to fill a position, the dynamics of relations and role responsibilities change slightly to reflect the added dimension of the new personality.

Since teachers and staff are at different stages in their professional development, the *training* needs for individuals must also be highly individualized. Training should match level of competence and professional interest. Otherwise, it may or may not be relevant to the needs of the individual.

Ongoing *evaluation* (both informal and formal) must also be an integral part of the administrator's role. Clear, honest, and helpful guidance and appraisal of performance is the best way to motivate individuals to excel.

All three legs of the performance triangle, *planning, training,* **and** *evaluating,* are intricately tied together. The hallmark of a successful program is that the flow of activity from one to another is constant. Individualized planning promotes purposeful training tailored to the needs of the person. This in turn necessitates regular evaluation to assess progress, which then provides the foundation for new plans and training procedures to keep step with the individual's professional growth.

Planning—breathing life into a job description

The joint planning conference provides a specific time when the director can sit down with each teacher to outline goals and strategies for performance. Directors who hold planning conferences, usually annually or semi-annually, feel that it builds rapport with each staff person because it allows them to work together to define possibilities for personal achievement.

Teachers need change. Hans Selye reminds us that "the human body, like tires on a car, wears longest when it wears evenly." Teachers need variety, new challenges, a fresh environment, and the opportunity to develop new interests and skills. The planning conference provides the opportunity for directors to share the broad vision they hold for the future of their centers, and to mesh the teachers' interests with the needs of the organization.

Most important, the joint planning conference is really a burnout prevention session because the emphasis of the meeting is positive and concentrates on the future. Director and teacher brainstorm together for creative ways to tap talent, channel energy, and keep that spark of enthusiasm burning.

But the joint planning conference is not a casual social affair. To the contrary, if the session is going to be productive, both director and teacher must prepare for it. When scheduling the conference, it is helpful to give the teacher some things to think about before the session.[16] These might be written out to help the individual clarify and isolate specifics that are important.

• What goals would you like to accomplish in the next six months? The next year?

• What areas of your job are you presently most satisfied with?

• What job responsibilities do you feel have need for improvement?

It will be useful as well to make copies of some of the self-assessment inventories in this book and also have on hand several fresh copies of the goal blueprint form on page 102.

Scheduling the planning conference just before the school term begins in early September is helpful because it will coincide with new hiring, changes in schedules, and assigned responsibilities. The session should last from one-half hour to two hours and take place in a quiet area of the school (or away from the center altogether) to insure that there are no interruptions. The length of the conference will depend on how long the teacher has been with the center and on the working relationship previously established with the director.

To be a successful session, the teacher should have primary control over the direction of the conference, with the director asking questions, giving feedback, and asking for clarification when necessary. Many teachers may need help moving away from generalizations when drawing up their goals blueprint. They may say, for instance, that their goal is to "become a more patient teacher" in the next six months. The director then becomes facilitator in helping teachers to define precisely those behaviors they hope to achieve.

The joint planning conference breathes life into the job description, making it a personalized, meaningful statement of the teacher's scope of responsibility. A good statement reflects the person's goals and aspirations for a specific period of time, and zeroes in on precise ways that those goals will be achieved and evaluated.

Working together to discover hidden talents, resources, skills, and interests can produce surprising results. At one center the director discovered that one of the teachers wanted to expand his budding talent in graphics and design work. The teacher had always done creative art projects with the children and produced some eye-catching bulletin boards, but he was ready to take on more challenging tasks. Together the director and teacher explored ways to juggle classroom responsibilities so that he could have time to coordinate the illustrations and artwork for the center's workshop flyers. The director gladly relinquished this task. The teacher received such glowing feedback, he even assumed the additional responsibility of co-ordinating the printing and distribution of the flyers.

Because planning and evaluation go hand and hand, the strategies outlined during the conference will provide the basis for later evaluation. The director and teacher decide together when and how evaluation should take place. Will the director or another staff member observe performance? Will a rating sheet be used? Will the teacher assess his or her own progress? Or will there be some tangible evidence, like a new curriculum guide or ten flannel board stories? Mutually agreeable standards for evaluating performance will help both director and teacher because monitoring and measuring achievement will be precise and not left to random subjective standards.

The most important question that the director can raise during the joint planning conference, however, is to ask, "In what ways can I support you in the next six months to help you achieve your goals?" Perhaps the teacher will ask for nothing more than resources and materials for specific units of study. But perhaps also the teacher may need more guidance, feedback, or help.

It is crucial that the session end with some kind of closure—a clear understanding of goals, objectives, expectations, and criteria for monitoring progress. A written work plan will become a useful tool during the training and evaluation of the teacher. One copy of this plan should be saved for the director and one kept by the teacher. To be sure, the first few times that teachers go through this planning sequence they will probably be over-ambitious in their hopes and aspirations for performance. But as the director gains skills in guiding the conference, individual goal statements will become more realistic and workable.

Joint planning conferences work. The investment of time and energy pays off in increased staff morale, better communication, and a more unified team approach. It is a step in staff development that cannot be ignored or shortchanged. Too much is at stake.

Joint Planning Conference

Staff person's name _____ Date _____

My work plan for the period _____

Goals and subgoals:

Game plan for achieving goals

1.

2.

3.

4.

5.

Resources needed for carrying out my game plan:

1.

2.

3.

4.

5.

Method of evaluation:

_____   _____
Staff Person   Director

Training—the critical match

From the joint planning conference, director and staff members have arrived at a mutual understanding of expectations, organizational needs, and the specifics of the job. The foundation has been laid for open communication and a good working relationship. But people need to have information, method, and techniques systematically communicated to them through a training program tailored to their individual stage of professional growth. The match is critical if we are to keep child care workers challenged, stimulated, and immune to the effects of stress and burnout.

When we look at the dynamics of training in a child care center, it is easy to focus our attention exclusively on the goal we want the individual to achieve, the mastery of a specific technique or skill. But training is not so much reaching a goal as it is a process. And it is that process that is so important in establishing motivation and feelings of competence and self-esteem in the individual worker. Viewing training as mostly process and only partly goal attainment changes the way in which we relate to people and the emphasis of our time and interactions with them.

Let us examine some of the ways that training can be tied to the different levels of professional growth and development of teachers in the early childhood setting. Lilian Katz, Director of ERIC/ECE, has suggested four stages of professional development of teachers that provide a useful framework for this discussion.[17] In each stage we shall also interject specific strategies for burnout prevention.

Stage 1: Survival is the name of the game. A child entering school for the first time must establish feelings of trust and acceptance before moving on to autonomy and initiative.[18] So, too, must the new teacher entering the early childhood teaching profession. The director's role in guiding this formative stage cannot be overemphasized. New teachers need support, encouragement, reassurance, and understanding.

This initial stage is vital in helping teachers develop specific competencies in the classroom as well as realistic expectations for measuring success and progress. It is a critical time to help them understand the importance of "pace" and develop specific strategies to cope with the demands of their new role. But directors are faced with a dilemma. How do we infuse a healthy dose of realism without dispiriting the new teacher? We want to keep individuals eager and enthusiastic, but we also want to insure that the initial burst of energy doesn't turn sour when idealistic expectations don't square with reality. Our goal must be to help new teachers remain committed and dedicated, yet at the same time develop a healthy perspective.

The first month on the job is important for building a foundation of trust and confidence in the director as a model. This is the time when new teachers are most eager to succeed, and will be open to suggestions about ways to improve. Time invested during this initial period demonstrating specific techniques and methods will really pay off later on.

This period is also important for helping new teachers become an integral part of the team, and feel that they are making a worthwhile contribution to group goals. A comprehensive staff manual is the best method of orienting new teachers to the specifics of the operation and over-all program goals and philosophy. However, only part of all that is shared with the new teacher in this early stage (both written and verbal) will be absorbed. Much of the information provided will seem irrelevant to new teachers and consequently only a small fraction of it will be internalized. But a well-written staff manual can serve as a good reference so new teachers can at least begin to develop an understanding of the nature of the operation.

The staff manual should include the following:

- school philosophy and goals statement
- relevant policies and procedures
- financial background of the center
- sample forms and reports to be filled out
- maintenance responsibilities
- list of where equipment and supplies are stored
- emergency procedures for fire, accidents, or natural disasters
- procedures for ordering supplies and materials

- payroll system, vacation, holiday and leave policy
- disciplinary and grievance procedures
- safety regulations, health requirements
- security procedures for the facility
- classroom guidelines for use of materials and equipment
- tips for successful parent conferences
- procedures for maintaining children's files and records
- staff roster
- relevant schedules, class lists, etc.
- job description of staff person

To help determine how successful we have been in guiding new teachers in the first month or so of their new roles, it may be useful to ask new staff to take a few minutes to fill out the following form. It will also convey to them that their impressions and opinions matter to you in your administrative role. The same form can be easily adapted to meet the needs of the individual classroom teacher who wishes to assess how aides and volunteers have been oriented to new classroom responsibilities.

Staff Orientation Assessment

Please take a few minutes to fill out the questions below. Your honest, candid responses will help us continue to meet the needs of new staff in our center.

1. Were you made to feel comfortable and welcome at the center on your first day on the job? Did other staff know you were coming?

2. Were you given enough familiarity with the particulars of our school environment to help you through those first difficult days (building, parking, lunch routines, restrooms, schedules, etc.)?

3. Were you shown where materials and equipment were stored and were procedures for snack, art, and the various curriculum areas made clear to you?

4. Were you given sufficient background on the school's policies, goals, and philosophy?

5. Were you made to feel that others had a personal interest in your progress, and did you feel as if you were a part of the group early on?

6. Was someone available to answer your questions when you were confused about particular procedures, or were you put in awkward predicaments because you did not have certain information necessary for you to perform your job?

Stage II: Consolidation. Having survived their first year in the child care center, teachers move into a new phase of their professional development. They have been through the cycle of new students, parent conferences, holidays, events, and activity units one time around. They feel more able to anticipate and plan, and are more psychologically prepared for their role.

Now they are ready to stretch a bit. They need to begin to apply what they have learned about children to new situations on their own. That is not to say that teachers in this stage do not want or need encouragement. But guidance and supervision should begin to move from the director to other experienced staff, peer group support becoming the dominant means of training for teachers at this stage of their development. In-service workshops, team teaching, and ample opportunities to work with one another in planning and implementing activities will not only spark enthusiasm but will build a strong unified team as well.

What teachers in this stage need more than anything else is to know that their directors have confidence in their ability to work through the resolution of problems. It is imperative, therefore, that directors exhibit a healthy tolerance for mistakes, allowing individuals to learn from their own repertoire of experience.

It is sometimes difficult to hold our tongues and not give advice on methods and techniques. But part of building autonomy and confidence in individuals means cultivating a willingness to take risks. Teachers must be allowed room to be less than perfect. It is critical, though, that this tolerance for mistakes be coupled with opportunity for teachers to discuss their problems and support one another in building independence and competency.

Stage III: Time for renewal. During the third and fourth years of working in the early childhood environment, teachers begin to tire of the same old routines and responsibilities. If variety isn't injected, stagnation will settle in and boredom result. Teachers in this stage of their professional development need to be recharged. They need to work with the director of their center to fully explore their many interests and find ways to generate more challenging responsibilities.

During this period it is particularly useful for teachers to visit other programs, attend conferences and workshops, and become active in professional organizations. Released time to take courses for an advanced degree or learn a new skill that could be applied in the school setting will help rejuvenate individuals, keeping them active and enthusiastic about their positions.

This is also the time when teachers benefit from taking on limited administrative responsibilities, becoming more active in coordinating materials and resources for the classroom. If the director is sensitive to the teacher's need for challenge, alternatives can be developed in the joint planning conference that will tap talents and keep teachers in this stage both interested and interesting.

At a planning conference at one center, for example, a teacher expressed the need for more variety in her responsibilities. On an experimental basis, she took on the job of coordinating a hot-lunch program for the children who had been bringing bag lunches. Not only did her new assignment add a gourmet touch to the children's menus, but it so inspired the other teachers that they began to take turns making the lunch, coordinating recipes, and compiling nutrition information for the school's newsletter. The experiment was so successful that several of the teachers sponsored a natural-foods cooking class for the parents of the center, and developed a cookbook of recipes for nutritious snacks for young children.

Stage IV: Maturity. There is always an element of risk involved in training. If directors are successful in developing teachers to excellence, after a period of time some of them—usually the most talented and successful—will move on. Once teachers have arrived at the stage in their development where there are no challenges left, it may be time for them to move on to new roles of responsibility. The administrator should genuinely feel proud of this departure. Breeding excellence and developing competence can only speak highly of the director's priorities.

Teachers who have arrived at this final stage in their professional development have a mastery of classroom methods, have achieved competence in teaching techniques, and are beginning to ask deeper questions about the philosophical and theoretical issues in education.

Occasionally there is a niche within the center that a teacher at this level of his/her career can assume. Leading workshops and seminars, coordinating teacher training, or assuming a major administrative role are some of the ways that individuals can continue to contribute to a school yet still feel personally challenged. But sometimes new challenges and professional growth can only come by leaving the center and moving on to a new position elsewhere. This can be a difficult, painful departure, but a necessary one, nevertheless, if the teacher is going to remain a committed, contributing part of the early childhood profession.

Evaluating—essential for continued growth

"To escape criticism, say nothing, do nothing, be nothing."
Sir John Simon

Evaluation is a natural extension of planning and training. It is a pivotal activity around which good directors manage programs for staff development. Evaluation lays the foundation for ongoing planning and the charting of new goals and objectives for individual performance. It makes us aware of what we do and helps us improve our behavior to become more effective in our designated roles.

Like training and planning, evaluation is a process. As such, it should be built into a good program and be constant and ongoing. Individuals who are working to improve performance need accurate information about how they are progressing. Evaluation supplies that information.

Since evaluation is so essential to good staff development, it is unfortunate that it has taken on such negative connotations. Many directors view the process as a royal headache at best, and often employees construe it as being arbitrary and threatening. This is because many centers rely on evaluating instruments that focus on "traits" and characteristics of the worker. When we try to evaluate "traits" such as co-operativeness, initiative, creativity, and thoroughness, we find that it is next to impossible to pinpoint what those qualities mean. Objectivity goes by the wayside. The evaluator ends up making an over-all performance judgment of the person and then rates all the specific trait items consistent with that judgment.[19]

A far more equitable approach is to view the process as a joint responsibility. Both the administrator and the child care worker sit down together to develop concrete standards and criteria for measuring performance. The attitude of both the director and the worker is remarkably different. There is no mystery in this approach. Both the director and the teacher know the standards and the methods that will be used for assessing progress.

The following are suggestions for the formal evaluation conference between the teacher and director. This conference should be held after three months with the new teacher and then at six month intervals for all staff. In centers that have established good staff development procedures, planning and evaluating with individuals takes place simultaneously. They recognize that if the performance triangle is in full motion, these functions are interdependent and flow together easily.

Focus on the future: If a teacher needs improvement, it makes little sense to dwell on the past. This seldom motivates individuals to improve their performance. Instead concentrate on the future and zero in on ways to achieve objectives that are clear and concise.

Evaluation should focus on behavior rather than on personal traits: Talking about abstract personal qualities is open to misinterpretation. Besides most traits really boil down to attitude, and there is little we can do to change a person's attitude. If we direct our comments instead to the person's performance as it relates to what they are doing, our chances for improving behavior are higher. As an individual's performance improves, so too will attitude.

For example, saying:

"It made me feel uncomfortable this morning when you didn't acknowledge Aaron's mother when she dropped off the carpool. It seemed she wanted to stay and observe in the classroom for a few minutes."

is more helpful than,

"You are insensitive to the needs of the parents in our center."

Evaluation should be specific rather than general: Direct comments to particular incidents or situations as they happen rather than to behavior in general. Keep it centered on your own observation rather than on inference or hearsay.

For example, saying:

"The windows in the staff room were not locked last evening and the lights were left on in the music room."

is more helpful than,

"You are not doing a good job closing up the center."

Evaluation should build on competencies of the individual: Feedback is most helpful if it focuses on the strengths of staff rather than their weaknesses. It sounds roundabout, but improving shortcomings is often best approached by concentrating on the person's positive abilities. Remediating deficits is an uphill struggle. Build on strength and potential instead.

Praise in public, criticize in private: Praise is not just the absence of criticism—it is a powerful tool for motivating individuals.[20] Acknowledging accomplishments and showing appreciation for hard work should be the cornerstone of all evaluation in an organization. People need recognition. They need to feel appreciated and to know they are valued. Genuine thanks is really a neglected form of compensation.[21] A bouquet of compliments can go a long way to increasing involvement and motivation.

Try not to couple praise with criticism: Telling a teacher, "You plan wonderful activities, but I think you need to improve the way you schedule them into the day," will probably only confuse him or her. In our attempt to be gentle, sometimes we couch

the negative in a veil of positive and hope this will motivate. But the approach usually backfires. The individual hears only the negative and focuses on that. Praise is a necessary ingredient in staff evaluation, but it should not be combined with criticism.

"Tact is the art of making a point without making an enemy."

When expressing dissatisfaction, be gentle, discreet and positive: If the purpose of evaluation is to help individuals improve, it does little good to alienate, intimidate, or make people defensive. Ordering, commanding, warning, or threatening have no place in organizations that value the integrity and rights of individuals. Besides, humiliating, blaming, or making staff feel guilty usually only produces resentment and resistence to change. Try to avoid using statements that begin with phrases like:

- *"You must . . ."*
- *"If you don't . . ."*
- *"You ought to try . . ."*
- *"I wish you would . . ."*
- *"I think you should . . ."*

Evaluation should not overload the circuits: Before the evaluation conference, think of the most important changes of behavior that you need to address. Then during the conference focus attention on as reasonable an amount that you feel the person can assimilate. If staff are bombarded with too much to think about and too many changes to make, the evaluation process will debilitate rather than motivate.

Evaluation does not mean giving answers and solutions: Evaluation means that director and teacher work together to generate solutions and explore alternatives. If an individual has a problem, don't let that person "give" the problem to you. Evaluating and giving feedback does not mean giving advice. It entails sharing ideas and helping individuals gain insight so that they can solve their own problems. Suggestions can be worded in a guiding form like, "Some teachers have found it helpful to. . ."

In centers where morale is high and teachers and directors have established a positive rapport, evaluation happens daily. On an informal basis the director gives feedback to workers so that they have a good idea of where they stand at all times—A brief chat to compliment a teacher on the way she handled an incident with a child, a quick follow-up to ask another teacher if the problem in the nap-room routine had improved, or a short note expressing thanks to a staff person who stayed overtime to cover or clean up. These are fairly insignificant as individual measures of evaluating performance, but over a period of time each individual accumulates sufficient feedback, so that when the formal evaluating conference rolls around there are no surprises and no startling revelations.

Tapping Staff as Partners in Decision-Making: Meeting the Need for Involvement

"When the best leader's work is done,
the people say, 'We did it ourselves."

Lao-tzu

An integral part of creating environments that enhance job satisfaction is respecting the need of individuals to have some say in the decisions that directly affect them. When involvement is broadened, optimism and hope rise commensurately, and energy and enthusiasm are unleashed. Moreover, when teachers are included in the formulation of program goals, they are more likely to be committed to achieving those goals.

This participatory approach to decision-making is central to burnout prevention in the child care environment. Considerable attention is being given to the entire area of participative management as a means of increasing productivity and worker satisfaction in other professions and industries as well. Indeed, as Professor William Ouchi so succinctly argues in his book, *Theory Z: How American Business Can Meet the Japanese Challenge,*[22] participative management is the dominant reason why Japanese industry has made such remarkable strides in the postwar decades. Mr. Ouchi contends that when employers practice openness, en-

courage skepticism, and strive to make their employees an integral part of the management team, the climate of mutual trust improves overall work relations. Absenteeism and turnover go down, efficiency and quality of performance go up.

The concept of participatory management is universal, however, and certainly applicable to the early childhood setting. When program administrators decentralize decision-making and increase staff input to maximum levels, involvement increases, morale is boosted, and worker motivation improved.

But the participative approach is not easy. It takes time to involve people, to communicate with them, and to keep them fully informed. Many directors are reluctant to open up channels for fuller participation because they have not learned effective techniques for increasing involvement. This is unfortunate, because the staff may interpret these actions as deliberate moves to keep the power and authority concentrated.

Those truly intent on expanding the sphere of involvement within their own organizations can take conscious moves to broaden input and awareness by staff. One small but significant step in this direction is to build in procedures whereby teachers and staff are kept fully informed about upcoming events, new procedures, or current activities. For example, teachers should get copies of newsletters, flyers, and informational letters being sent home before they get distributed. There is nothing quite so frustrating for a teacher than to be asked by a parent about an event, policy, or activity about to take place that the teacher knows nothing about. Teachers need to feel that they are on top of the current situation if they are to be effective in their role of helping parents. Nobody likes to feel helpless and uninformed.

Directors seeking to gradually expand participation can also examine the full scope of decisions involved in the operation of the center, look at the consequences of those decisions, and isolate just how the decision-making process is affecting people on the staff. The possibilities for decision making generally fall into three categories: Those best made by the Board or the program director only; those that should be made by the teachers exclusively; and those that can be made with the combined input of teachers and administration. These will vary according to the expertise, abilities, and interest of the director and staff, as well as the organizational structure of the individual center.

Directors who are sensitive to the importance of staff involvement will look carefully at these last two categories of decision-making, for this is the area that can generally be expanded to increase participation at the staff level. For example, the arrangement of space and materials in the classroom, detailing of work scheduled, and assignment of rotating responsibilities can all be made co-operatively with teachers, or possibly turned over to them entirely if they are ready for that level of decision-making. Even involving teachers in the hiring of new staff or inviting their input to the Board on policies that affect them will do much to increase feelings of involvement and improve over-all morale.

An example of how the process might work occurred at one center that had switched from a half-day to a full-day care program. The administrator, in a effort to accommodate the schedules of working parents, changed the school calendar so that the center operated a full twelve months, observing only a few holidays. The psychological consequences on teachers was demoralizing. At a staff meeting the teachers expressed the need for a definite beginning and end to their job responsibilities—even if it was just a two or three-day period at the end of August when the center was closed for cleaning, revitalizing, and planning for the new group of children. The following year the director notified the parents that the center would be closed for a week in June and a week in late August. Tuition was adjusted accordingly and the parents were able to find alternative care for their children during that time because they had been given sufficient notice. The psychological boost to the staff was felt immediately. Morale was much higher because they could anticipate a fresh beginning and plan on a sense of closure at the end.

Just because we deem it worthwhile does not mean that we will easily achieve our goal of fuller participation, however. Our zeal to increase involvement and staff motivation must be tempered with good judgment. The dynamics of any child care organization are intricate and behaviors cannot be changed overnight. Fuller participation is a learning and growing process for both director and staff. Achieving greater involvement takes time and must be assimilated into the organizational structure *gradually*. In many cases, patterns of behavior and interrelationships in the decision-making process are well established, even well entrenched, in the very heart of the organization. Involvement and changes cannot be thrust on people.

How do administrators go about opening channels for increased involvement without disrupting the continuity of the program, and preserving the good aspects of the organizational decision-making process as they presently exist? First, the director must become informed, know how individuals view the organization, and actively solicit feedback about ways to improve conditions. Second, the director can begin to apply changes in the decision-making process through well organized and constructive staff meetings. These can become the focal point for building team spirit and a cooperative approach to the management of the center. The remainder of this section will be devoted to a fuller discussion of these two methods for expanding participation.

Building awareness by soliciting feedback

Changes and innovation are the lifeblood of enriching experiences in early childhood education. But innovation is not so much something completely new as it is a new twist on the old. Find new solutions to old problems is what creativity is all about. In most centers, though, coming up with creative ideas is not the problem. What is the problem is the willingness of those in charge to be open and receptive, and to actively solicit suggestions for change.

Walter Lippmann once said, "In organizations where everyone thinks alike, no one thinks very much."[23] But cultivating diversity by generating feedback from staff is a step many directors are reluctant to take. This is usually because their perspective is narrow and focused on the present. Why rock the boat? Why get people to think about change when the status quo is so comfortable? This attitude neglects the long-term accumulative impact on the morale of individuals as well as the collective group of teachers.

Not only does staff input increase the possibilities for creative decision-making, but it has a salutary effect as well. When teachers are able to give feedback, question procedures, suggest alternatives, and exchange differing points of view, morale among staff is usually boosted. Individuals are offered a legitimate way to aid the institution before frustrations take root and cause job complacency or job dissatisfaction. Moderate "griping" can be healthy, as long as it is channeled toward improving conditions.

The most important kind of feedback an administrator or head teacher can solicit is informal and acquired daily. This requires finely tuned listening and communicating skills, as well as a sensitivity to the body language and nuances of behavior that convey messages about how individuals feel about their work environment.

Sometimes, despite our best efforts, teachers (particularly new ones) feel uncomfortable speaking up about an issue. By virtue of our position, it may be difficult to get certain individuals to open up. We might have to provide opportunities through direct questions to demonstrate our willingness to listen. A few door-openers that might help to open up this exchange are:

- "Can I help you in any way?"
- "I'd like to know how you feel about . . ."
- "Would you like to talk about . . ."
- "How are things going with your group?"
- "Is there anything that I can do to help?"

But directors and teachers also need to weave in methods of formal feedback to demonstrate the seriousness with which opinions are accepted. This may coincide with the individual staff person's evaluation or planning conference, but in many settings a more formal written procedure is the best method to solicit true feelings and opinions about the organization. This procedure should definitely be included in a year-end wrap-up where objectives are reevaluated, and whenever a staff person leaves the employment of the center. Some also feel that they would benefit from distributing a feedback questionnaire midway through the school term.

Directors should use two different feedback forms, one for staff and one for the parents of the children attending the center. Together they will provide a realistic assessment of the director's performance in balancing the needs of staff, children, and parents. Only in this way will directors be able to identify strengths and weaknesses in their leadership style and work to improve their effectiveness.

The following are sample feedback questionnaires used at an early childhood center that has both a half-day and full-day program. The questions covered may give you some ideas to include in your own feedback questionnaires for your center or for your individual classroom.

Staff Feedback Questionnaire

Dear Staff:

Every once in a while it is important for me to stand back and assess whether or not we are all reaching and striving for the same goals and objectives in our program, or if there are areas that I have somehow neglected to focus attention on. I need your honest, candid feedback if I am going to weave all our diverse needs and interests into a unified approach in our center. Feel free to talk to me personally about any additional areas that I might not have covered on this questionnaire.

1. What do you see as being the collective philosophy that moves this school?

2. As a teacher, do you feel you are a unique and special person that is valued and respected as a part of our staff?

3. Does working at this school enhance you or drain you as an individual?

4. Do you feel that communication is open and that other staff understand and respect your position and viewpoints?

5. In what ways do you feel that we might be able to improve the program for children?

6. What suggestions do you have for improving schedules, routines, and procedures that you have been involved in?

7. How do you assess the effectiveness of our staff meetings? Are there areas that we should try to incorporate into future meetings?

8. What did you appreciate most about your year working on this staff?

9. What did you appreciate the least about this past year in your position?

> Thank you for caring enough to share your ideas and feelings with me.

Parent Feedback Questionnaire

Dear Parents,

We have always relied heavily on suggestions from the parents of our students for new ideas and ways that we might improve our program. It would be most helpful to us, therefore, if you would take a few minutes of your time to answer the questions below. Return your completed form to the school office.

Thank you for your support.

1. In what ways has your child benefited from the learning experiences provided here at our center?

2. Do you feel that there are any areas that have been neglected?

3. Do you feel that you as a parent have benefited from the center? Have our newsletters, workshops, lectures and parents' library helped you in your parenting role?

4. What other services should we be providing?

Thank you!

Making meetings count

"A camel is a horse designed by a committee."

Meetings can be the most powerful tool that directors have for tapping the creative energy of their staff and fostering greater involvement in decision-making. If run poorly, though, meetings can be a waste of time, a waste of dollars, and a real source of tension among staff. It is unfortunate that many child care workers view meetings as time where nothing gets accomplished and participants end up feeling frustrated, bored, or even resentful. At the same time, though, most recognize that meetings are absolutely essential for creating a unified team approach to managing a center.

Meetings don't have to be unproductive and frustrating. There are specific methods that administrators can implement to plan and conduct successful meetings.[24] The skills involved take patience and practice to achieve. But the payoff is well worth it because it can have a remarkable effect on the degree of cohesion that binds a group together and the spirit in which teachers relate to one another.

The following tips and techniques should be helpful in developing purposeful meetings in your own center.

Visualize what you hope to accomplish during the meeting: In general terms, we hope that individuals come away from a meeting with a better understanding of themselves and others and the issues that surface during the meeting. On a more specific level, however, directors who plan a meeting should have a concrete idea of precisely what they hope to accomplish. For example, they may want participants to implement a new procedure in the classroom, to generate ideas for a fundraiser, or to express their viewpoint on a new policy being considered. Whatever the objective, it needs to be clearly defined at the outset in order to structure the meeting to achieve the desired outcome.

Decide what format the session will follow: Once objectives are clear, the format that the meeting will follow should fall in place. There are four different approaches typical of staff meetings of early childhood programs.

First there is the *information-sharing* session. Here the director or meeting facilitator presents ideas, clarifies policies, and provides staff with opportunities to ask questions and discuss information necessary to run the program.

Second, there is the *instructional* format where new skills, techniques, and procedures are explained and demonstrated. Most in-service workshops are of this variety. For example, a specialist might demonstrate how to use a new set of musical instruments or a Red Cross volunteer instruct certain first-aid procedures.

Third, there is the *brainstorming* format. At this session, ideas are actively solicited from participants on how to solve a particular problem. Brainstorming begins by defining the problem as precisely as possible—the who, what, where, and when of the issue. The next step is to describe the conditions that will exist when the problem is solved. Then teachers are invited to generate as many different solutions as possible for resolving the problem. No discussion or evaluation of the ideas takes place yet, for the purpose of such a session is to create a nonjudgmental atmosphere that encourages individuals to toss out as many alternatives as possible. The brainstorming session may end at this point if further study is needed to assess alternatives. Or it can lead into a decision-making sequence to narrow down to the best possible solution.

The fourth format is the *decision-making* meeting. Here participants are called upon to make a decision between presented alternatives. The director may structure this kind of session as "I need your help in arriving at a final decision about . . ." and provide the information and data necessary for the staff to arrive at a consensus of the direction to take. Later, as the group assumes a more active role in the decision-making process, they can gradually take on the responsibility of gathering the information necessary as well as making the final decision.

These different formats are not mutually exclusive. Certain staff meetings will include all four types. Other meetings will concentrate on one. The reason for providing this framework is to help the leader determine the purpose and type of interaction so that objectives can be met.

Select the appropriate participants for the meeting: Many times when individuals complain about meetings it is not so much that the meeting was run poorly or even that the content of the session was organized poorly, only that there was a mismatch in the content and participants selected to attend. All who attend the meeting should have a distinct purpose for being there. If items are going to be discussed or procedures demonstrated that don't really apply to every person, the meeting should be restructured to allow those people the opportunity to leave early, arrive late, or not attend at all. We must respect the way that we structure staff members' time and insure that it is meaningful and purposeful.

Perhaps the cost-benefit approach of evaluating meetings is the best way to guarantee that all the individuals that are attending any given meeting should be attending. Stop and total up all the dollar hours being spent at a particular session. Does the content of the meeting justify it? When looking at the composition of the meeting participants, consider their expertise, their interest in the topics addressed, and interpersonal communication skills. This will give a clearer picture of how the dynamics of the meeting might unfold and whether or not objectives for the meeting will be met.

The size of the group must also be manageable for the tasks anticipated. If the meeting is of an information-sharing or instructional type, twenty or possibly more people could be accommodated. But if the meeting is a session for brainstorming or decision-making, more than twelve participants can inhibit participants from making contributions to the discussion. The ideal number will depend on many factors, including the familiarity of participants with one another and the leader's skill in achieving full participation. But the organizer must be aware of these many influences to structure as conducive a setting as possible to achieve the objectives of the meeting.

Schedule the meeting for the right time: The frequency and time of the staff meeting will depend on the needs of the center and the working relationship of the participants. However, if communication channels for feedback and full participation are to be kept open, regular staff meetings are essential. Regular means weekly in many centers. But just as important is that the meetings be held at a consistent time when all the staff can prepare for it. In this way they will know what to expect. Meetings planned for the same time each week also make it easier to schedule in parents or aides to supervise the children during the meeting if necessary.

Begin and end the meeting on time: The most productive meetings are scheduled for one hour to one and one-half hours. They consistently start and end on time. The importance of beginning and ending a meeting on time cannot be overstated. If we want to convey to individuals that we respect them, it is imperative that we take into consideration that they are busy people with many responsibilities and better things to do than wait around for meetings that are late in starting or drag on interminably.

The way to begin on time is to begin on time regardless of late arrivals. If administrators wait until everyone has arrived, those who arrived on time will feel penalized and begin to be tardy for future meetings. Also, it is important not to reward late arrivers by going over items they have missed. Some directors also make a point of noting in the minutes who was there when the meeting began and who arrived late.

Sometimes it is possible to discourage tardiness by scheduling a habitual latecomer first on the agenda. Others find that by scheduling meetings for unusual times (1:10), people are more prompt. If we expect others to arrive on time, it is crucial that we have ready all the essentials to conduct the meeting before people arrive. Chairs, chalkboards, pencils, markers, paper, and projectors need to be assembled ahead of time.

Ending a meeting on time can sometimes present as many problems. A clock strategically placed on the table or visible to all participants is one way to help, but the real responsibility for ending on time belongs to the meeting leader. If teachers and staff know that meetings do in fact end when they are scheduled to, they will be far more attentive and not as likely to stray from agenda items.

Think about the environment where the meeting will take place: A previous section of this book elaborates on the psychological importance of space on the dynamics of group interactions. Being sensitive to those principles may determine whether or not the administrator is successful in achieving full participation by staff at meetings. Giving careful thought to the seating arrangement to facilitate good eye contact between all participants is a must in planning a successful meeting. Circular arrangements, for example, often promote feelings of unity and discourage side conversations.

In setting up the meeting room, eliminate potential distractions so that participants can keep their full attention on the topics. Directors should also look at the overall comfort level of the room in terms of light, heat, and ventilation. It may be necessary as well to have a parent or aide cover the telephone during the meeting, or insure that an automatic answering device records messages until the session is over. There is nothing quite so disconcerting than to have the momentum of a good discussion destroyed by the ring of a telephone.

Since meetings also serve the function of creating a social network among staff, think of ways to make participants feel comfortable with one another, increasing rapport. Providing coffee, tea, and a snack will help relax people. Individual name tags can help break the ice for a new group. A small vase of flowers can also add a special touch to the occasion.

Develop an agenda for action: Much of the success of any meeting is determined before it actually begins. The agenda, distributed beforehand, determines how well prepared individuals come to discuss specific issues, as well as the tone of the meeting itself. A well-thought-out agenda serves as the group's road map. It provides a sense of direction and gives participants concrete guidelines to structure their discussion.

The best agendas are developed jointly by staff and administration. Careful attention has been given to the order of the items to be covered and the length of time that each item should be discussed. The agenda includes the date, place, and starting and ending time of the meeting as well as particulars about the items to be considered so that individuals will bring necessary papers, reports, and other relevant data.

The director must also look at each suggested topic and determine if a meeting is the best way to address the issue. In some cases, the information can best be covered by a written memo with meeting time reserved for follow-up discussion only. This in itself can save a great deal of time. The director may also decide that a particular topic can be handled best by part of the staff meeting separately, that smaller group then reporting to the full staff meeting.

To be effective, agendas must be distributed before the meeting, preferably a full day or two. Careful attention should be given to the way individual items are described on the agenda. The language should be straightforward and concise as well as positive in tone. There is no "correct" way to structure the order of items to be considered. Only experience with a particular group can determine how discussion will flow. But starting the meeting off on a good note can set the tone for the entire session, so thought must be given to which item should be discussed first. Also, people tend to be more alert during the early part of a meeting so this is the time to schedule items of high priority.

The following form is a useful sample for organizing your meetings.

Staff Meeting Agenda

Date of meeting: _October 18_   Place of meeting: _staff room_

Participants: _Georgia, Karen, Bev, Laurie, Mike, Cindy, Jeff, Sandy_
Sharon, Bill

Beginning time: _1:15 pm_   Ending: _2:30 pm_

Please bring the following: _One Halloween poem/fingerplay or activity to_
share + one recipe for nutritious lunch or treat to be included in #5 on agenda

Agenda Item	Format	Person Responsible	Time Allocated	Action Taken
1. Halloween shar-a-thon	information sharing	all	5 minutes	
2. Update on enrollment changes and group assignments	informational	Sandy	15 minutes	
3. Update on T-shirt fundraising sales	informational	Georgia	5 minutes	
4. Discussion of possible guest speakers for spring lecture series	brainstorming	Jeff	10 minutes	
5. Compile written guidelines for parents sending bag lunches to school with their children	brainstorming decision-making	Sandy	30 minutes	
6. Demonstration on how to use new fire extinguisher. Review of evacuation procedures for fire drill.	instructional	Georgia	10 minutes	

Staff Meeting Agenda

Date of meeting: _____   Place of meeting: _____

Participants: _____

Beginning time: _____   Ending: _____

Please bring the following: _____

Agenda Item	Format	Person Responsible	Time Allocated	Action Taken
1.				
2.				
3.				
4.				
5.				
6.				

Guide the discussion to include all participants: The role of facilitator during a meeting is perhaps one of the most challenging tasks of managing people. To a large extent, the degree of participation and cohesion that develops in a staff rests on how well the director guides the involvement of teachers during the staff meeting. Each participant should feel that the opinions and ideas they have expressed have been listened to fairly. But it is a fine art indeed to create the right balance so that no one dominates discussion and all feel free to express their viewpoints.

Particularly with a new group of teachers who have not yet established a close working rapport, it is often difficult to get them to open up and talk. One method used in some centers is to begin the meeting with a round-robin sharing. Each participant takes five to ten seconds to answer a question that was posted prior to the start of the meeting. These questions are only intended to break the ice, not to be springboards for a full-blown discussion. Some possibilities:

- What is one incident you handled with a child this week that made you feel proud?
- What is one good thing you observed another teacher do this week that you would also like to try out?
- Name one pet peeve you have about the way space is organized in the classroom?
- What was the nicest thing a parent said to you last week?
- What are your two favorite children's books?

Some directors find that by allowing just five to eight minutes of time at the beginning of the meeting where each teacher can quickly tell others about a new resource, field trip idea, classroom management tip, or curriculum activity that they have recently tried can really open up involvement. But the guidelines for this kind of flash starting must be structured and uniformly adhered to or the purpose of the exercise will be lost.

Another way to facilitate involvement is to rotate the leadership role. This provides good experience for others in managing and organizing people; it allows the director to play a less visible role which in itself might make some teachers feel less inhibited about expressing their viewpoints; and it gives the person filling in as group facilitator an appreciation of how difficult it is to balance the needs of all the participants and still accomplish the business before the group. This may make the person a more cooperative and contributing participant in the future.

If the director's role as facilitator is to stimulate discussion, it is best to stay away from questions that can be answered with a simple yes or no. Open-ended questions will have better results in getting people to explain their positions. The director must also exercise care to be an attentive listener, resisting the urge to talk too much. Allowing time for people to reflect is also important. Many groups feel embarrassed at any silence, yet it is necessary to build in a cushion of silent space occasionally so that people will not feel pressured.

A sense of humor also helps individual participants feel more at ease in a group setting. Meetings tend to get very serious and the ability to keep things lively by injecting humor when appropriate can take the edge off an otherwise tense moment.

Finally, the director facilitates discussion by clarifying, reiterating, and summarizing comments so that all have a clear understanding of what has been decided. Wrapping up each item before moving on to the next topic also helps people develop clear expectations of what they are supposed to do as a follow-up and by when.

Being an effective facilitator does not automatically happen. It requires patience and practice and sensitivity to nonverbal signals. The director senses when members feel discouraged, frustrated, confused, or just plain bored, and redirects the discussion to keep up the pace. Leadership must be flexible, adapting to the needs of the group and altering the agenda if necessary to keep involvement and interest high.

Follow up the meeting with recorded minutes: Most directors· of child care centers do not have the time or the secretarial support to type up elaborate minutes. But it is important, nevertheless, to provide a written summary of the highlights of the staff meeting. This information refreshes memories and helps inform those who could not attend.

One way to achieve this written summary is to assign one person to serve as recorder during the meeting. The job of recorder can be rotated each week. As agenda items are completed, the recorder briefly describes in the Action Taken column on the form any information that should be preseved. This record can then be posted the following day or duplicated and distributed to individuals who could not attend. Copies of this "complete" agenda also allows directors to look back, see trends, and assess progress over the years.

Centers that have more than seven or eight staff attending a meeting may want the recorder to record the proceeding on a chalkboard or newsprint flip chart. This record can capture the basic ideas brought up and serve as a visual aid in recalling particulars during and after the meeting.

Checklist for Effective Staff Meetings

	Yes	No
1. Were all participants informed of time with a written agenda?	___	___
2. Did the meeting start on time?	___	___
3. Did the meeting begin on a positive note?	___	___
4. Was the room arranged to facilitate good interaction between staff?	___	___
5. Was the content of the meeting relevant to all participants?	___	___
6. Did the group have enough background, information, and expertise to make necessary decisions?	___	___
7. Did all participants have a chance to express their opinions and offer suggestions if they wanted to?	___	___
8. Was the facilitator successful in keeping the discussion focused and on track?	___	___
9. Did the facilitator talk too much?	___	___
10. Did the facilitator restate, summarize, and achieve a consensus of understanding on one issue before moving on to the next?	___	___
11. Was there sufficient time allotted for each item scheduled?	___	___
12. Did the facilitator allow enough room and flexibility to adapt the agenda to the needs of the group?	___	___
13. Was the facilitator able to guide discussion so that it did not get bogged down in trivia or turn to petty gossip?	___	___
14. Did the meeting end on a positive note?	___	___

References and Suggestions for Further Reading

Chapter 1: Job Burnout in Early Childhood Education

Notes

¹ There are three action-oriented organizations whose efforts should be commended in this area. First, the *National Association for the Education of Young Children* (NAEYC) has already made impressive strides in increasing public awareness of the issues. Through its annual conferences, monthly journal and advocacy work, it remains an important avenue for implementing change. The ambitious efforts of the *Child Care Information Exchange* are also particularly noteworthy. This professional journal has consistently highlighted topical articles on administrative and employee issues. As a forum for exchanging information, it serves as an excellent vehicle for addressing job burnout and stress-related concerns. A third group whose enterprising efforts have received considerable national attention is *The Child Care Staff Education Project*. This organization received a grant from the Rosenberg Foundation to publish a national newsletter and establish a clearinghouse for information on ways to enhance child care services and improve staff working conditions. Readers interested in learning more about their activities may write to the Child Care Staff Education Project, P.O. Box 5603, Berkeley, California 94705.

² Diane Ryerson and Nancy Marks, "Career Burnout in the Human Services: Strategies for Intervention." Paper delivered to the American Psychological Association Annual Meeting, 1981.

³ Christina Maslach and Ayala Pines, "The Burn-Out Syndrome in the Day Care Setting." *Child Care Quarterly*, Summer 1977, pp. 100–113.

⁴ J. B. Rotter, "General Expectancies for Internal Versus External Control of Reinforcement." *Psychological Monographs 80*.

⁵ Maslach and Pines, op. cit. p. 109.

⁶ Abt Associates, *Children at the Center*. Final Report of the National Day Care Study, Cambridge, Massachusettes, March 1979. Child Care Staff Education Project, *Who's Minding The Child Care Workers?: A Look At Staff Burn-Out*, Oakland, California, 1980. National Association for the Education of Young

Children (NAEYC) Early Childhood Staff Salaries Task Group, *Report to the Governing Board*, November 1979.

[7] Abt Associates, op. cit.

[8] U. S. Department of Labor, *Bureau of Labor Statistics: Employment Perspective: Working Women*, Report No. 574, No. 2, April-June, 1979.

[9] Child Care Staff Education Project, op. cit.

[10] Anne Lewis, "Teacher's Salaries: Hard Times Ahead," *Learning*. March 1981, p. 28–31.

[11] Stephen Truch, *Teacher Burnout*, Novato, California: Academic Therapy Publications, 1980, pp. 22–26.

[12] Jere E. Yates, *Managing Stress*, New York: AMACOM, 1979, p. 19.

[13] Hans Selye, *Stress Without Distress*, New York: Signet Books, 1974.

[14] Yates, op. cit.

[15] Daniel Girano and George Everly, *Controlling Stress & Tension: A Holistic Approach*, Englewood-Cliffs, N. J.: Prentice-Hall, Inc., pp. 37–50.

[16] Hans Selye, *Stress of Life*, New York: McGraw-Hill Book Company, 1976.

[17] Yates, op. cit., p. 29–30.

[18] Alvin Toffler, *Future Shock*, New York: Bantam, 1970. *The Third Wave*, New York: William Morrow and Co., Inc., 1980.

[19] Richard Hough and Dianne Fairbank, *Journal of Health and Social Behavior*, 17: 70–82, 1976.

[20] Thomas H. Holmes and Richard Rahe, "The Social Readjustment Rating Scale," *Journal of Psychosomatic Research*, 11: 213–218, 1967.

[21] Girano, op. cit., pp. 113–117.

[22] Meyer Friedman and Ray Rosenman, *Type A Behavior and Your Heart*, New York: Fawcett Crest, 1974.

[23] Drawing the conclusion, however, that all "workaholics" are prime candidates for burnout would be erroneous. In her

book, *Workaholics*, (Addison-Wesley, 1980), Marilyn Machlowitz reports that some workaholics are surprisingly happy and able to lead productive, stress-free lives despite their devotion to work.

[24] Friedman, op. cit., p. 10.

[25] Jay Rohrlich, *Work and Love: The Crucial Balance*, New York: Summit Books, 1980, p. 17.

[26] The material for this section was adapted from Girano and Everly's research on the biochemical causes of stress as reported in their book, *Controlling Stress & Tension*, op. cit., pp. 91-97.

[27] John Kenneth Galbraith, *The Age of Uncertainty*, Boston: Houghton Mifflin Company, 1977.

[28] Techno/Peasant Survival Team, *The Techno/Peasant Survival Manual*, New York: Bantam Books, 1980. Projecting how technological advances will affect our way of life in the coming years is a popular topic for many writers. Another particularly insightful glimpse into the future is a powerful paperback by Christopher Evans titled *The Mighty Micro*, London: Coronet Books, 1979.

[29] Yates, op. cit., pp. 42-43.

[30] Friedman, op. cit., pp. 194-195.

[31] Herbert Benson, *The Relaxation Response*, New York: William Morrow and Company, 1975, p. 17.

[32] Ellen Goodman, "Plight of the Mother-Woman," *Washington Post*, April 9, 1981.

[33] Ryerson, op. cit.

[34] Marvin Greenberg, "The Male Early Childhood Teacher: An Appraisal," *Young Children*, January, 1977, pp. 34-38.

[35] Paul Liberatore, "A Pre-school Where the Teachers Are Male," *Independent Journal*, San Rafael, California, September 2, 1977.

[36] Joel I. Milgram and Dorothy Sciarra, "Male Preschool Teacher: The Realities of Acceptance," *The Education Forum*, January, 1974, pp. 245-248.

[37] Reducing the sense of isolation that male teachers experience is the goal of a newsletter specifically geared to men in early childhood education. *Nurturing News* can be ordered by

writing to David Giveans, 187 Caselli Avenue, San Francisco, California, 94114. In association with *Total Video*, Giveans, has just released a new movie on the subject as well. Rental/purchase information on *Men in Early Childhood* can be obtained by writing directly to Mr. Giveans.

[38] Toffler, *The Third Wave*, op. cit., p. 35.

[39] Ryerson, op. cit.

For further reading

Bryan, William. "Preventing Burnout in the Public Interest Community." *Northern Rockies Action Group Papers.* Vol. 3, No. 3, Fall, 1980.

Cichon, D. J., and Koff, R. H. "Stress & Teaching." *NASSP Bulletin* (1980), pp. 91–104.

Coates, Thomas J. and Thorasen, Carl E., "Teacher Anxiety: A Review with Recommendations," *Review of Educational Research,* Spring 1976, vol. 46, no. 2, pp. 159–184.

Edelwich, Jerry and Brodsky, Archy. *Burn Out: Stages of Disillusionment in the Helping Professions.* New York: Human Sciences Press, 1980.

Freudenberger, Herbert. *Burn Out: The High Cost of High Achievement.* Garden City, New York: Doubleday & Company, Inc., 1980.

Hendrickson, Barbara. "Teacher Burnout: How to Recognize It: What to Do About It," *Learning.* January 1979, pp. 36–39.

Levinson, Harry. *Executive Stress.* New York: Signet. 1964.

Mattingly, Martha. "Sources of Stress and Burn-Out in Professional Child Care Work," *Child Care Quarterly.* Volume 6, No. 2, Summer 1977.

Neugebauer, Roger. "Why Do Directors Burn Out?" *Child Care Information Exchange.* September 1979.

Potter, Beverly A. *Beating Job Burnout.* San Francisco: Harbor Publishing, Inc., 1980.

Seiderman, Stanley. "Combatting Staff Burnout," *Day Care and Early Education.* Summer 1978.

Sheehy, Gail. *Passages: Predictable Crises of Adult Life.* New York: Dutton, 1974.

Venniga, Robert and Spradley, James. *The Work/Stress Connection.* Boston: Little Brown & Company, 1981.

Chapter 2: Self-Assessment

Notes

[1] John Kotter, *Self Assessment & Career Development*, Englewood Cliffs, New Jersey: Prentice Hall, 1978, p. 7.

[2] Particularly helpful for compiling the information in this section of biological rhythms was *Controlling Stress & Tension*, (Prentice-Hall, 1979), by Daniel Girano and George Everly. The authors provide a variety of self-assessment tools that help the reader recognize and reduce stress.

[3] Philip Goldberg and Daniel Kaufman, *Natural Sleep*, New York: Bantam Books, 1978, p. 93.

[4] This quote comes from Richard Bolles best-selling book, *What Color Is Your Parachute* (Ten Speed Press, 1978). Bolles puts a strong emphasis on self-assessment as a crucial step in determining the appropriate match between the individual and his/her career voice. The approach certainly underscores the preventative measures that can be taken by all job-seekers to avoid burnout caused by a mismatch in expectations.

[5] Margaret Hennig and Anne Jardin, *The Managerial Woman*. New York: Simon & Schuster, 1977. pp. 210–213.

[6] Wayne Dyer, *Pull Your Own Strings*. New York: Avon Books, 1978, p. 154.

[7] Lilian Katz, "Teaching in Preschools: Roles and Goals," *Children*, March/April, 1970, Vol. 17, No. 2, p. 43.

For further reading

Glasser, William. *Reality Therapy*. New York: Harper & Row, 1965.

Ferner, Jack. *Successful Time Management*. New York: John Wiley & Sons, Inc., 1980.

Jacobson, Edmund. *You Must Relax: Practical Methods for Reducing the Tensions of Modern Living*. New York: McGraw Hill, 1975.

Mattlin, Everett. *Sleep Less, Live More*. New York: Ballantine Books, 1979.

Pembrook, Linda. How to Beat Fatigue. New York: Avon Books, 1975.

Sheehy, Gail. *Pathfinders.* New York: William Morrow & Company, 1981.

Wofford, Joan. "Know Thyself—The Key to Improving Your Leadership Style," *Child Care Information Exchange*, November, 1979.

Chapter 3: Managing Time

Notes

[1] Jay Rohrlich, *Work and Love: The Crucial Balance*, New York: Summit Books, 1980, p. 146. Rohrlich tells of one Indian culture that has defined its basic unit of time as the time it takes to boil rice. Anthropological literature is replete with colorful descriptions of the various ways that people around the world and throughout history have interpreted time concepts in their social structures. In Hindustani, for instance, the word "Kal" means "tomorrow." But it also means "yesterday." In our cultural context this sounds illogical. However, in India, where time is universal and unchanging, individual dates have no real significance. In the context of Hindu timelessness, the concept is readily understood. The variations in the way different cultures symbolize the time experience is important because the extent to which a culture agrees on its temporal language has a bearing on how well social behavior is coordinated within that culture.

In his book, *The Harried Leisure Class*, (New York: Columbia University Press, 1970), Staffan Linder also points out that time conventions have another useful function in our understanding of the way we use and experience time. They can be directly linked to technological development and economic status of a group of people. In this analysis there are essentially three categories of defining the structure of time:

Cultures with a *surplus* of time can be found in the poorest countries around the world. Productivity is so low that it creates forced idleness. In fact, the whole notion of measuring time as we know it does not exist because the need to measure, calculate, and use time wisely does not exist. The mañana attitude is prevalent in these cultures. The need to plan the future revolves around such concepts as "the dry season" or "when the moon is full." In some areas of the Middle East, the structure of time is so informal that all events occurring beyond a week are lumped into one broad category that denotes the future.

Cultures with a slightly more developed economy occupy a middle ground in which the supply of time is *affluent*. Here as economic growth progresses and the level of income rises, so too does the need to utilize and measure time more precisely. In these cultures, there seems to be enough time. Appointments remain casual, leisure time is ample, and the pace of activity moderate and relaxed. Certain aspects of rural America fit into this group.

The final category of time orientation, as it relates to economic status of culture is the one with which we are most familiar. *Time-famine* cultures have the highest standard of income by western standards and the greatest scarcity of time. Awareness of time, in fact, permeates every aspect of social behavior. The clock is often viewed as a tyrant, and all possible slack in the use of time has been eliminated. Punctuality is a virtue, and squandering time is scorned.

[2] Mark Stein, *How to Make Time Work for You, The T Factor*, New York: Playboy Paperbacks, 1976, pp. 4–7.

[3] Meyer Friedman and Ray Roseman, *Type A Behavior and Your Heart*, New York: Fawcett Crest, 1974, p. 231.

[4] I am indebted to Kenneth J. Jaffe of the International Child Resource Institute for his help in developing this goals blueprint. The Institute assists agencies and organizations in formulating goals, conducting needs assessments and implementing effective strategies for fundraising and child advocacy.

[5] Peter Drucker, *Management Tasks, Responsibilities, Practices*, New York: Harper & Row, 1973, pp. 43–48.

[6] Merrill Douglass and Donna Douglass, *Manage Your Time, Manage Your Work, Manage Yourself*, New York: AMACOM, 1980, pp. 73–77. The authors have developed a very useful matrix for distinguishing the importance and urgency of items to be done. Exercise 22 was adapted from this strategy of prioritizing time.

[7] Bertrand Russell, *In Praise of Idleness*, London: Unwin Books, 1960, p. 18.

[8] William Glasser, *Positive Addiction*, New York: Harper & Row, 1976.

[9] Helen Reynolds and Mary Tramel, *Executive Time Management*, Englewood Cliffs, New Jersey: Prentice-Hall, Inc., 1979, p. 107.

[10] Joan Koob Cannie, *Take Charge*, Englewood Cliffs, New Jersey: Prentice-Hall, Inc., 1980, p. xiv.

[11] Margaret Hennig and Anne Jardin, *The Managerial Woman*, New York: Simon & Schuster, 1977, p. 47.

[12] Edwin Bliss, *Getting Things Done*, New York: Charles Scribner's Sons, 1976, p. 100.

[13] Douglass, op. cit., p. 241.

[14] Bliss, op. cit., p. 124.

For further reading

Ellis, Albert and Knaus, William. *Overcoming Procrastination*. New York: Signet Books, 1977.

Fensterheim, Herbert and Baer, Jean. *Don't Say Yes When You Want to Say No*. New York: Dell Publishing, 1975.

Ferner, Jack. *Successful Time Management*. New York: John Wiley & Sons, Inc., 1980.

Lakein, Alan. *How to Get Control of Your Time and Your Life*. New York: New York: Signet Books, 1973.

LeBoeuf, Michael. *Imagineering*. New York: McGraw Hill, 1980.

Lee, John W. *Hour Power*. Homewood, Illinois: Dow Jones-Irwin, 1980.

Mackenzie, Alec. *The Time Trap*. New York: McGraw Hill, 1970.

Mackenzie, Alec and Waldo, Kay. *About Time: A Woman's Guide to Time Management*. New York: McGraw Hill, 1981.

Neugebauer, Roger. "Managing Time, Your Most Precious Resource," *Child Care Information Exchange*, February, 1979.

Parris, Crowley A. *Mastering Executive Arts and Skills*. West Nyak, New York: Parker Publishing Company, Inc., 1969.

Porat, Frieda. *Creative Procrastination*. San Francisco: Harper & Row, 1980.

Scott, Dru. *How to Put More Time in Your Life*. New York: Rawson, Wade Publishers, Inc., 1980.

Turla, Peter A. *Effective Time Management*. San Francisco: National Management Institute, 1979.

Chapter 4: Managing Space

Notes

[1] Theodore Caplow, *How To Run Any Organization*, Hinsdale, Illinois: Dryden Press, 1976, pp. 82–84.

[2] John DeLorean, *On a Clear Day You Can See General Motors*, New York: Avon Books, 1979, pp. 19–36.

[3] It is interesting to note that environmental psychologists learn much about how humans operate in space by observing the way animals relate in space. While we must be cautious about making direct parallels to human behavior from the data generated from animal study, research into these areas does provide helpful insights into certain aspects of human behavior.

In his book, *Personal Space* (Englewood Cliffs, New Jersey: Prentice-Hall, Inc.), Robert Summer points out that in the animal kingdom, dominant species tend to have larger personal space than those which occupy lower positions in hierarchy. One need only look at the expansive domains of the eagle, the lion, or the whale for obvious examples. But even in the barnyard, the top chickens have greater freedom of space and can walk anywhere, leaving lower chickens restricted to smaller areas. In human society, social and spatial orders also correlate. The social elite possess more space in the form of larger homes and have greater spatial mobility by opportunities to travel. This is in marked contrast to the small spatially-restrictive environments of public housing for low-income groups.

Territoriality is another concept in the study of animal environmental behavior that seems to have application to human behavior. Territoriality insures the propagation of the species by regulating density. It offers protection from predators, a safe home base for breeding, and protection against over-exploiting any part of the environment that the species depends on for its survival. Humans, too, have territoriality needs, and have invented ways of defending what they consider their turf. "A man's home is his castle" is a phrase we often hear. We've constructed an elaborate labyrinth of laws to guard our territorial rights, including prohibitions on unlawful search and seizure, trespass, and removal or destruction of property. We have also made very clear distinctions between private property, the exclusive domain of individuals, and public property, the collective territorial domain of a group.

In the study of crowding, many animal research experiments have also produced valuable insights for human environmental psychology. Well known for his studies, for example, is the ethologist John Calhoun. He conducted studies spanning fourteen years in which he monitored the effects of crowding on the behavior of Norway rats. Crowding, he found, can disrupt social functions and lead to disorganization, aggression, and ultimately to population collapse or large-scale die-off.

[4] Concepts like personal space, territoriality, and crowding must be put in a cultural context as well. Edward Hall calls this the "hidden dimension" of space (*The Hidden Dimension*, Garden City, New York: Doubleday & Co., 1969), because cultural systems play a powerful role in shaping behavior based on different sensory perceptions of the world. Perhaps the most obvious examples of cultural differences in space concepts are the wide variations in how individuals throughout the world define their "space distance," the socially accepted distance between interacting people. Much of what regulates socially accepted behavior is a tacit respect for established spatial norms within each culture. We often use expressions like "keeping someone at arm's length" or that something was "too close for comfort" as ways of defining our personal space distance. But what is "accepted" distance really depends on the context of the situation and the players involved.

Our spatial patterns are by no means universal. Touching, social interactions, and the size of our "personal space bubble" vary around the world from culture to culture. In fact, much of the physical discomfort that Americans experience in dealing with foreign cultures stems from a difference in perception of spatial norms.

Arab cultures, for instance, have a far higher tolerance for crowding in public places than Americans or northern Europeans. The pushing and shoving in public places characteristic in many Middle Eastern countries is not being pushy or rude. It merely comes from a different set of assumptions about how people interact with one another in a given space. The entire experience of space is also quite different in traditional Japanese culture. When Americans think and talk about space, we generally mean distance between objects. We perceive space as empty and react to the arrangements of objects within an area. Japanese, in contrast, are trained to give meaning to various spaces. They perceive the shape and special characteristics of individual spaces far differently than we do. They even have a special word, ma, to convey this idea. The ma, or interval, is the essence of Japanese spatial experience. It relates to everything in Japanese culture from flower arrangements to ornamental gardening, to the order and serenity implicit in the layout of living environments.

[5] Sybil Kritchevsky and Elizabeth Prescott, *Planning Environments for Young Children: Physical Space*, Washington, D.C.: National Association for the Education of Young Children, 1969, pp. 4–6.

[6] Ibid, p. 42.

[7] Perhaps the most comprehensive study available of the spatial considerations of early childhood environments is the two-volume guide written by Gary Moore and associates of the Center for Architecture and Urban Planning Research at the University of Wisconsin in Milwaukee. Titled *Recommendations for Child Care Centers* and *Recommendations For Child Play Areas,* these resources are highly recommended for architects and educators designing new facilities or renovating existing structures. Both were extremely helpful in compiling the information in this section.

[8] John Ott, a pioneer in this field, has done some important studies linking the effects of environmental light on the hyperactive behavior of children. He has concluded that classroom lighting may be a factor. Under improved lighting conditions using "full-spectrum" fluorescent tubes with lead-foil shields over the cathode ends to stop x-rays from escaping, some children's

behavior showed dramatic improvement. See "Influences of Florescent Lights on Hyperactivity and Learning Disabilities," *Journal of Learning Disabilities*, Aug./Sept. 1976, and *Health and Light*, New York: Pocket Books, Simon & Schuster, Inc., 1976.

⁹ Robert Bartholomew, *Child Care Centers: Indoor Lighting, Outdoor Playspace*, New York: Child Welfare League of America, Inc., 1973, p. 6.

¹⁰ Celia Decker and John Decker, *Planning and Administering Early Childhood Programs*, (2nd edition), Columbus, Ohio: Charles E. Merrill Publishing Company, 1980, p. 139.

¹¹ *"Blue is Beautiful,"* *Time Magazine*, September 17, 1973, p. 66.

¹² Bartholomew, op. cit., p. 7.

¹³ Decker, op. cit., p. 139.

¹⁴ Elizabeth Jones, *Dimensions of Teaching—Learning Environments*, Pasadena, California: Pacific Oaks College, 1977, pp. 4-6.

¹⁵ Decker, op. cit., p. 133.

¹⁶ Moore, op. cit., p. 409.

¹⁷ Moore, op. cit.

¹⁸ The reader may find the following two resources particularly helpful in creating classroom learning environments that promote prosocial behavior and foster important skills and concept development in young children:

Thelma Harms, *Early Childhood Environment Rating Scale*, New York: Teachers College, Columbia University, 1980. This is an easy-to-use evaluation for rating early childhood settings. It has been produced at the Frank Porter Child Development Center at the University of North Carolina at Chapel Hill after extensive field testing and assessment by early childhood educators.

Diane Trister Dodge, *Room Arrangement as a Teaching Strategy*, Washington, D.C.: Creative Associates, 1978. This filmstrip and cassette tape narration are particularly helpful as a guide in arranging interest centers in the classroom.

¹⁹ Kritchevsky, op. cit., p. 19.

For further reading

Abramson, Paul. *Schools for Early Childhood.* New York: Educational Facilities Laboratories, 1970.

David, Thomas G. and Wright, Benjamin, editors. *Learning Environments.* Chicago: University of Chicago Press, 1974.

Dean, Joan. *Room to Learn.* New York: Citation Press, 1974.

Douglass, Merrill and Douglass, Donna. *Manage Your Time, Manage Your Work, Manage Yourself.* New York: AMACOM, 1980.

Evans, E. Belle. *Designing A Day Care Center.* Boston: Beacon Press, 1974.

Gibson, David. "Down the Rabbit Hole: A Special Environment for Preschool Learning," *Landscape Architecture Magazine,* May, 1978.

Gross, Dorothy, "Equipping a Classroom for Young Children," *Young Children,* December, 1968.

Grossman, Lee. *Fat Paper.* New York: McGraw-Hill, 1976.

Harms, Thelma. "Evaluating Settings for Learning," *Young Children,* May, 1970.

Haase, Ronald. *Designing the Child Development Center.* Washington, D.C.: Project Head Start, U.S. Department of Health, Education, and Welfare, 1969.

Jones, Elizabeth. "Creating Environments Where Teachers, Like Children, Learn Through Play," *Child Care Information Exchange,* 1979.

Mackenzie, Alec and Waldo, Kay. *About Time: A Woman's Guide to Time Management,* New York: McGraw Hill Book Company, 1981.

Marzollo, Jean. "Spaces and Places for Everything," *Learning Magazine,* Sept., 1978.

Osmon, Fred Linn. *Patterns for Designing Children's Centers.* New York: Educational Facilities Laboratories, 1973.

Prescott, Elizabeth. "The Physical Environment—A Powerful Regulator of Experience," *Child Care Information Exchange,* April, 1979.

Reynolds, Helen and Tramel, Mary. *Executive Time Management.* Englewood Cliffs, New Jersey: Prentice-Hall, Inc., 1979.

Scott, Dru. *How to Put More Time in Your Life.* New York: Rawson, Wade Publishers, Inc., 1980.

Sanoff, Henry and Sanoff, Joan, *Learning Environments for Children.* Raleigh, N.C.: Learning Environments, 1972.

Winston, Stephanie. *Getting Organized.* New York: Warner Books, 1978.

Chapter 5: Managing People

Notes

[1] Joe Batten, *Expectations & Possibilities*, Reading, Mass: Addison-Wesley Publishing Company, 1981.

[2] Robert Townsend, *Up the Organization*, New York: Fawcett Crest Books, 1970. p. 116.

[3] Ibid.

[4] Joan Koob Cannie, *Take Charge: Success Tactics for Business and Life*, Englewood Clifs, New Jersey: Prentice-Hall, Inc., 1980, pp. 101–102.

[5] Douglas McGregor, *The Human Side of Enterprise*, New York: McGraw Hill Book Company, Inc., 1960.

[6] Roger Neugebauer, "Motivating Your Staff," *Child Care Information Exchange*, April, 1979.

[7] Abraham Maslow, *Motivation and Personality*, (second edition), New York: Harper and Row, 1970.

[8] Frederick Herzberg, *Work and the Nature of Man*, New York: World Publishing Company, 1966. Frederick Herzberg, "One More Time: How Do You Motivate Employees?" *Harvard Business Review* 46(1): pp. 53–62. Henry Murray, *Explorations in Personality*, New York: John Wiley & Sons, 1938.

[9] Nathaniel Stewart, *The Effective Woman Manager*, New York: John Wiley & Sons, 1978.

[10] Margaret Hennig, *The Managerial Woman*, New York: Simon & Schuster, 1977, pp. 44–45. Joan Koob Cannie, *The*

Woman's Guide to Management Success, Englewood Cliffs, New Jersey: Prentice-Hall, Inc., 1979, p. 7.

[11] Vince Lombardi, quoted in *Bits and Pieces,* Gregory Marvin, editor, Fairfield, New Jersey: The Economics Press, Inc.

[12] Celia Decker and John Decker, *Planning and Administering Early Childhood Programs,* (2nd Edition), Columbus, Ohio: Charles E. Merrill Publishing, Co., 1980, p. 93.

[13] John Samaras, quoted in "Make Communications a Two-Way Street," by Roger Neugebauer, *Child Care Information Exchange,* November, 1980.

[14] Robert Louis Stevenson, quoted in *Writing With Precision,* by Jefferson D. Bates, Washington, D.C.: Acropolis, 1978. This is a superb guide for any teacher or administrator who seeks to improve writing skills.

[15] Peter Drucker, *People and Performance,* New York: Harper & Row, 1977, p. 58.

[16] Thomas Gordon, *Leader Effectiveness Training,* New York: Bantam Books, 1977, p. 251.

[17] Lilian Katz, "Developmental Stages of Preschool Teachers," *Elementary School Journal,* 1972, 73(1), pp. 50–54.

[18] Erik H. Erikson, *Childhood and Society,* (revised edition), New York: W. W. Norton and Company, 1964.

[19] Gordon, op. cit., p. 240.

[20] Decker, op. cit., p. 94.

[21] Townsend, op. cit., p. 170.

[22] William Ouchi, *Theory Z: How American Business Can Meet the Japanese Challenge,* Reading, Mass.: Addison-Wesley Publishing Company, 1981.

[23] Bill Schul, *How to Be an Effective Group Leader,* Chicago: Newson-Hall, 1975., p. 2.

[24] Michael Doyle and David Straus, *How to Make Meetings Work,* New York: Playboy Paperbacks, 1976. This is a very thorough guide on the dynamics of group meetings and was particularly helpful in compiling the information in this section.

For further reading

Caplow, Theodore. *How to Run Any Organization.* Hinsdale, Illinois: Dryden Press, 1976.

Cudaback, Dorothea. "Meetings That Work," *Human Relations Newsletter,* University of California Cooperative Extension Service, September, 1980.

Cherry, Clare. "Promoting Harmonious Staff Relationships," *Child Care Information Exchange,* January, 1980.

Drucker, Peter. *Managing for Results.* New York: Harper & Row, 1964.

Farson, Richard. "Praise Reappraised," *Harvard Business Review,* 1963, No. 5, pp. 61–66.

Hewes, Dorothy. "Leadership in Child Care—What Contingency Theory Can Show Us," *Child Care Information Exchange,* January, 1981.

Lilian Katz. *Helping Others To Teach.* Urbana, Illinois: ERIC/ECE, January, 1979.

La Crosse, E. Robert. "Thoughts For New Administrators," *Young Children,* September, 1977.

Lehner, George. "Aids for Giving and Receiving Feedback, *Child Care Information Exchange,* June, 1978.

Neugebauer, Roger. "Ideas for Effective Meetings," *Child Care Information Exchange,* February, 1979.

Neugebauer, Roger. "Are You An Effective Leader?" *Child Care Information Exchange,* January, 1979.

Pokras, Sandy. *Managing Staff for Results.* Oakland: The Viability Group, 1978.

Sciarra, Dorothy. *Developing and Administering A Child Care Center.* Boston: Houghton Mifflin Company, 1979.

Van Maanen, John. "The Process of Program Evaluation," *Grantsmanship Center News,* Jan./Feb., 1979.